THE WEEKEND QUILTER

FABULOUS QUILTS TO MAKE IN A WEEKEND

Edited by Rosemary Wilkinson

NEW HOLLAND

This edition first published in the UK in 1997 by New Holland Publishers (UK) Ltd

London • Cape Town • Sydney • Auckland

24 Nutford Place	80 McKenzie Street	3/2 Aquatic Drive	Unit 1A, 218 Lake Road
London W1H 6DQ	Cape Town 8001	Frenchs Forest, NSW 2086	Northcote, Auckland
United Kingdom	South Africa	Australia	New Zealand

10 9 8 7 6 5 4 3

Created and produced by Rosemary Wilkinson Publishing
4 Lonsdale Square, London N1 1EN

ISBN 1 85368 930 0 (hardback)
ISBN 1 85368 931 9 (paperback)

Art editor: Sara Kidd
Illustrator: Carol Hill
Photographer: Marie-Louise Avery
Copy editor: Michèle Clarke

Reproduction by Hirt and Carter (Pty) Ltd
Printed and bound in Singapore by Tien Wah Press (Pte) Ltd.

CONTRIBUTOR PROFILES

PAULINE ADAMS
was one of the team operating the The Quilter's Guild of Great Britain's quilt documentation programme and contributed to the resulting book, "Quilt Treasures". She has written a number of articles in 'The Quilter' magazine and her own book on patchwork. She exhibits regularly at national and local shows.

JENNI DOBSON
is a regular contributor to national patchwork magazines and has been teaching and demonstating patchwork at major European events since the late 1970s. Her quilts have won rosettes at major British quilt shows and were selected by The Quilters' Guild for their fourth and fifth national exhibitions.

CAROL DOWSETT
has taught City & Guild Creative Studies Patchwork courses for many years. As a founder member of The Computer Textile Design Group, she has been involved in developing the use of computers for design into textiles in secondary schools. Her computer designed hangings are exhibited nationally and in the rest of Europe.

GILL TURLEY
works as a freelance speaker and teacher of quiltmaking. The Quilters' Guild selected her quilts to include in their national exhibitions in 1987, 1991 and 1993 and photographs of her quilts have featured in several recent quilt books. She has been a member of the Executive Committee of The Quilters' Guild since 1991.

ANNE WALKER
originally trained as a mathematics teacher and has always had a great interest in geometric designs. She is a prominent member of The Quilters' Guild. She has been involved in setting up the curriculum for a national patchwork course and has written and contributed to other patchwork books. She currently runs a patchwork and quilting supplies business, "Piecemakers".

CONTENTS

QUICK QUILT TECHNIQUES 6
Anne Walker

QUICK Quilt TECHNIQUES

DEVELOPMENT OF TECHNIQUES

The art of quiltmaking has been with us for many generations. Quiltmaking techniques were first brought to British shores by the crusaders who found the technique much in use in the Middle East. By the time of the Victorian era it was an established art form in many households. It was at this time that the skilled needlewoman demonstrated that she was indeed an artist and a designer, piecing together intricate designs from an array of wonderful fabrics. Much of the patchwork done at this time was either the rich "Crazy Patchwork" in sumptuous fabrics, embellished with stitches and beads, or geometric piecing, simple geometric shapes stitched over papers before being joined together with a whipping stitch. This latter method has come to be known as "English Paper Piecing".

In America the pioneer women developed a technique that has become an American art form, the "Patchwork Block"; this enables quiltmakers to piece their quilts in small units before assembling the quilt top. The revival of patchwork in Britain in the 1970s was very much based on these blockmaking techniques.

If we look at many patchwork quilt patterns they can be broken down into smaller units consisting of strips, squares and triangles. For decades these shapes have been cut using templates and pieced either by hand or machine. Such templates have been an invaluable tool for the patchworker, and indeed still are when more intricate shapes are used. However, modern lifestyles often demand a quicker approach. The advent of the rotary cutter has enabled the process to be speeded up, allowing the quiltmaker to achieve pleasing results in a much shorter time scale, for example in just a weekend. All the quilts in this book are quick projects in which the pieces are cut with a rotary cutter and machine pieced. They allow the reader to be creative in the time available, however short.

QUILT SIZES

A favourite and versatile quilt size is between 54 in and 60 in/135 cm and 155 cm square, which can be used for a baby – as a wrap, a play-rug, cot quilt and even for a while as a single bed quilt – or for an adult as a lap quilt. Larger square quilts can be used as throws. The book also features rectangular quilts for use as pram and cot quilts, single bed quilts, throws or as elegant wall-hangings.

FABRICS
Selection

Selecting fabric for a project is a personal thing. Each of the projects included is made in the maker's own choice and it is clear to see that quiltmakers develop a unique style and taste. Some are made from soft flannels and brushed cottons to produce warm and comforting quilts, others are made from cottons, resulting in bright colour arrangements suitable for display or for interior decorations. In each of the five sections suggestions have been given for different colourways for one of the quilts.

Your fabric choice will stamp your individuality on the project. It is never possible to recreate a quilt exactly, as fabric designs and colourways are always changing. To achieve interest in your quilt you need to use different tonal values and if you are using print fabrics, the scale of the print is also an important factor. The tonal values of fabric in your quilt should include light, medium and dark fabrics. These values are relative to each other, so one person's medium may be another person's light; the fabrics can even play different roles in the same quilt. If you are unsure of the value of the fabrics, you can view them through a value finder, a red screen that eliminates the colour and allows you to see the lightness and darkness, i.e. the value. A similar effect can be achieved by photocopying fabric and looking at the value of the greyness. Another technique that you can employ is to stare at the fabric selection and gradually squint at it: the darker fabrics "disappear" first. This is a good technique when perhaps you are confused between brightness and lightness.

Equipment for the quick quilter: an acrylic ruler; a bias square; a set square; a rotary cutter and mat; a "BiRangle"; a hand-held hoop; various marking pencils and quilting threads and a selection of fabric pieces.

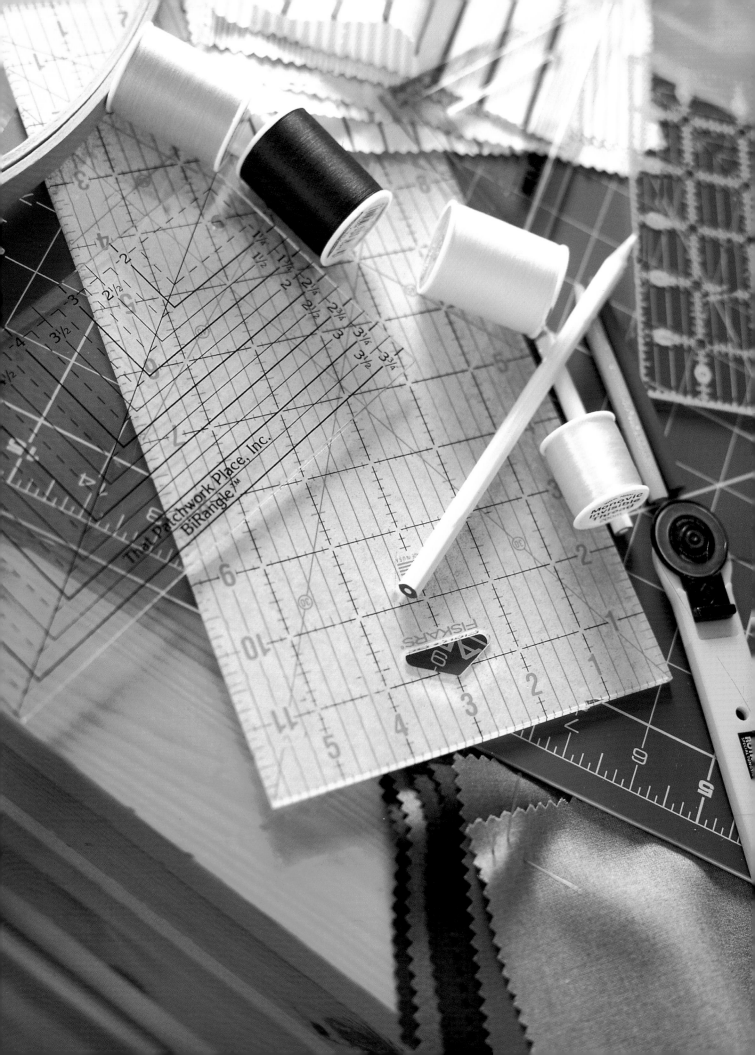

The scale of the design of a print fabric is very important. Try to use a variety of scales – small prints when viewed from the distance will look like solids. Your quilt needs to hold interest both close to and from a distance. Geometric designs add movement, encouraging the eye to move over the surface and allowing you to see the other fabrics. There are also fabrics on the market now that are self-coloured prints or textured solids which are good substitutes for a solid fabric, giving a softer overall finished look.

You can always experiment with colouring a quilt design on paper before making your fabric selection, but remember no coloured pencil or felt tip pen can recreate a single fabric or its effect when placed next to another. If you are unsure of your fabric selection, purchase only a small amount and try a fabric mock-up. Quiltmakers are avid collectors of fabric, often buying without a project in mind. These fabrics can be used for some of the projects in this book; if, however, you plan to purchase additional fabrics, do take the existing ones along with you to see them all together. It is very difficult to carry an image of colour in your head and finally, always be prepared to change your mind.

All the fabric sizes in this book give a margin for error, so that you can purchase fabric with confidence. Most rotary cutting projects involve the cutting of strips first; these are best cut from across the width of fabric. Therefore, take care if a design calls for a quarter: most quilting supply shops sell quarters either "fat" or "long". A long quarter is cut 9 in/25 cm deep by the width of the bolt. A fat quarter is cut 18 in/50 cm deep by the width of the bolt, then split at the fold to give a piece 18 x 22 in/50 x 56 cm. Only buy a fat quarter if the design specifies such a size.

PREPARATION

All the fabric for your project must be washed separately to ensure that excess dye is removed. You do not need a detergent but the water needs to be hot. Keep rinsing until the water runs clear, which may take several rinses. If you wish to use the washing machine and have no means of collecting the waste water to check for dye, place a piece of white cloth in the machine together with the fabric. If the dye bleeds, it will do so into the white cloth. Repeat the process until no more dye runs. If dye continues to run after repeated washes, you may feel that you have to abandon this fabric. It is not advisable to try setting the dye with salt or vinegar, as it will only set it until the next wash and if you intend to wash your quilt, the colour will run throughout the quilt. Separate instructions are given within the book for fabric preparation if you are dyeing it yourself.

After washing, partially dry, then iron the fabric while still damp to replace its original crispness. Press with the selvages together just as it came off the bolt.

ROTARY CUTTING
Equipment

There are lots of different pieces of rotary cutting equipment on the market. You will need the following basic set for the quilts in this book:

Acrylic ruler. This should be a purpose-made rotary ruler with a non-bevelled edge. Never use metal rulers, as they will ruin the blades of your rotary cutter. Markings should be on the underside of the ruler and should be laser printed and easy to read. Beware of any ruler with the markings on the top surface; this leads to a parallax view of the measurements, which will not be accurate. Any angles marked on the ruler should be marked in both directions. A good size to have is 6 x 24 in/15 x 60 cm.

Bias square. This special tool will aid the cutting and squaring up of half square triangle units. A good size to have is 6 x 6 in/ 15 x 15 cm.

BiRangle. This tool (see page 143) is marked with a grid designed to help you to stitch rectangles twice as long as they are wide. When the rectangles are cut from contrasting strips that have been stitched together, you can quickly and accurately make long, thin pairs of triangles.

Rotary cutter. These come in different sizes: small, medium and large. A good size to have is the medium, which is classed as heavy duty. The small one is good for trimming and for cutting curves. The large one is excellent for cutting large multiple layers but if you are a newcomer to the techniques, this is slightly more difficult to control. Cutters come with a safety cover which should be engaged at all times when you are not cutting. Also make sure that they are stored safely, out of reach of children. Safe habits prevent accidents from happening. Replacement blades are readily available. Keep your cutter well maintained: blunt blades will ruin your mat as well as making cutting difficult and unpleasant.

Self-healing rotary cutting mat This is essential. Do not cut on any other surface. The mats come in a variety of sizes: a good size is one on which the fabric will fit with only one fold. The boards come with a grid on one side. This grid is roller printed and is not always accurate, so do not rely on it for measurements. To avoid confusion you could always use the reverse side of the board.

Set square. This is for straightening up the fabric before cutting. A second rotary cutting ruler will substitute for this.

All this equipment, except for the "BiRangle", is available with either imperial or metric measurements.

Measurements

All measurements are given in both imperial and metric. Fabric allowances are interchangeable for the purpose of buying the required fabric. However, all cutting instructions are not. Use either imperial or metric: do not mix the two.

The seam allowances (unless otherwise stated) are $\frac{1}{4}$ in if you are working in imperial or 0.75 cm if working in metric. Although 0.75 cm is bigger than $\frac{1}{4}$ in, these seam allowances work well with the rotary cutting equipment. All cutting instructions already include seam allowances, therefore you will not need to add any extra. However, if you adapt any of the quilts or create your own designs, it is worth remembering the following when calculating seam allowances:

Imperial
seam allowance: $\frac{1}{4}$ in
cutting strips/squares/rectangles: add $\frac{1}{2}$ in
cutting half square triangles: add $\frac{7}{8}$ in
cutting quarter square triangles: add $1\frac{1}{4}$ in

Metric
seam allowance: 0.75 cm
cutting strips/squares/rectangles: add 1.5 cm
cutting half square triangles: add 2.5 cm
cutting quarter square triangles: add 3.5 cm

Diagram 1 shows how these additions are calculated.

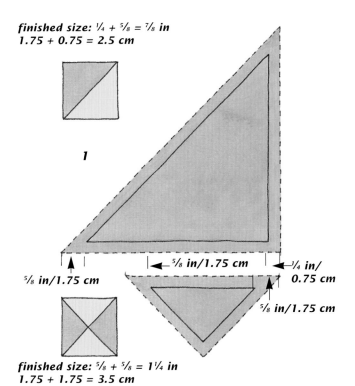

finished size: $\frac{1}{4}$ + $\frac{5}{8}$ = $\frac{7}{8}$ in
1.75 + 0.75 = 2.5 cm

1

$\frac{5}{8}$ *in/1.75 cm* $\leftarrow \frac{5}{8}$ *in/1.75 cm* $\leftarrow \frac{1}{4}$ *in/ 0.75 cm*

$\frac{5}{8}$ *in/1.75 cm*

finished size: $\frac{5}{8}$ + $\frac{5}{8}$ = $1\frac{1}{4}$ in
1.75 + 1.75 = 3.5 cm

Creating a straight edge

Regardless of how well the fabric was originally cut, you will have to straighten the edge before cutting pieces for your quilt, in order to produce accurate strips across the fabric.

1 Place your fabric on the cutting mat with the fold towards you and the selvage away from you and all the surplus fabric to the side in the direction of the hand you cut with. Make sure that the selvages are exactly aligned.

2 Lay a set square on the fold of the fabric and line your ruler up against the square with a horizontal line on the ruler in line with the bottom of the square (diagram 2).

2

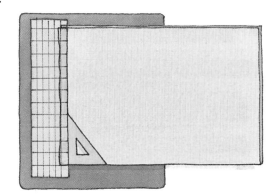

3 Place your hand at the bottom of the ruler, remove the set square and, starting cutting in front of the fold in the fabric, cut until your cutter is level with the top of your hand, then maintaining the pressure on the cutter, creep your hand further up the ruler, cut again and repeat the process until you have finished cutting off the waste strip (diagram 3).

3

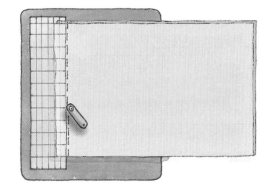

Cutting strips

This is the first stage to produce strips cut crosswise across the fabric, either to be used as they are or to be cut again to produce squares, rectangles and triangles.

1 Fold the fabric in half, so that the fold lies on top of the selvages and the cut edges lie together (diagram 4). There are now four thicknesses of fabric.

4

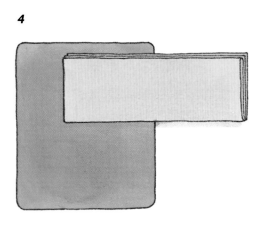

2 Place the ruler on your fabric with a horizontal line on the fold and the desired width measurement on the straightened edge (diagram 5).

5

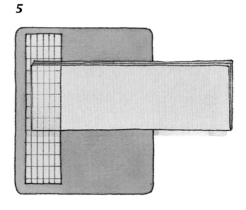

3 Place your hand firmly in the centre of the ruler, start cutting before the fold and cut across the fabric in one movement.

4 Repeat until you have cut the number of strips needed. Open out the strips and check that they have straight edges. If they have a slight "V" shape, or if it becomes difficult to line up the ruler with the horizontal on the fold and the measurement along the whole cut edge, repeat the process to create a straight edge given on page 9.

Cutting squares

1 Cut strips to the desired width as described above.

2 Pick up the fabric with the double fold in your cutting hand and turn until it is horizontal on the board. Straighten up the end with the single fold and selvage (diagram 6).

6

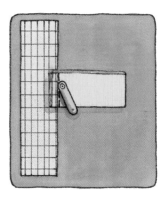

3 Using the same measurement as the initial strip, cut into squares, making sure a horizontal line on the ruler is on the bottom edge of the fabric (diagram 7). This process is called **sub-cutting**.

7

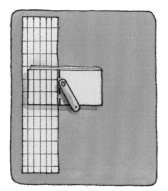

Cutting rectangles

1 Cut strips to the width of one of the measurements of the rectangle as described above.

2 Turn the strip for cutting again, straighten the end and sub-cut using the second measurement of the rectangle.

Cutting measurements wider than ruler

A second ruler or square can be used to aid the cutting of wider strips (diagram 8).

8

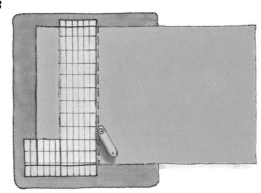

Cutting half square triangles

1 Cut strips to the desired measurement, including the seam allowances.

2 Turn the strip for sub-cutting as before, straighten the end and cut a square.

3 Pivot the ruler until it lies exactly across the diagonal of the square. Cut into triangles (diagram 9).

9

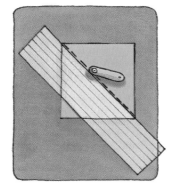

4 Repeat steps 2 and 3 until you have sub-cut the required number of half square triangles.

Cutting quarter square triangles

1 Cut strips to the desired measurement, including the seam allowances.

2 Turn the strip for sub-cutting as before, straighten the end and cut a square.

3 Pivot the ruler until it lies exactly across one diagonal of the square and cut.

4 Without moving the pieces, pivot the ruler the other way until it lies exactly across the other diagonal of the square, and cut (diagram 10).

10

5 Repeat steps 2 to 4 until you have sub-cut the required number of quarter square triangles.

Cutting stitched strips

1 Lay the strips across the board with the surplus length towards the hand you cut with.

2 This time when trimming or sub-cutting, line up a horizontal line on the ruler with one of the seams instead of with the lower edge of the fabric.

MACHINING
Setting up the machine for stitching

Start each quilt with a new needle. If you will be sub-cutting stitched strips, the stitch length needs to be shorter than for normal stitching. A guide is to stitch at 12 stitches to the inch/ 5 stitches to the centimetre.

For an accurate quilt top, the seam allowance that you stitch must also be accurate, you cannot just trust in the width of your presser foot. To ensure an accurate width, work as follows:

1 Take a piece of graph paper either marked in quarter inches or in millimetres and cut the right-hand edge of the paper so that you have a line exactly ¼ in/0.75 cm from the edge.

2 Place this paper under the presser foot and stitch with the stitches on the line.

3 Stick a piece of masking tape on the bed of your machine along the edge of the paper. (Alternatively there are magnetic stitching guides that you can place on the machine up against the edge of the paper.)

4 Remove the paper and you are ready to stitch. It is always advisable to stitch a test piece first. Cut three short pieces of fabric 1½ in/4.5 cm wide. Stitch the three strips together along the long sides into a block, butting the fabric against your stitching guide. Press the seams away from the centre strip, then measure between the seam lines on the right side. If you are accurate, this measurement will be 1 in/3 cm. If it is in any way out, set up your guide again and re-test.

MACHINE PIECING

Machine piecing always appears to use an endless supply of thread, so before starting a project, fill several bobbins in readiness.

Chain-piecing is a method that speeds up the whole process: stitch two pieces together, leave them under the presser foot, then butt up the next pair. Continue stitching and butting up the following pairs until you have stitched all the pieces (diagram 11).

A third piece can be added to these two in the same way (diagram 12) and the process can be repeated as often as you like. Snip the pieces apart when you have finished.

11   *12*

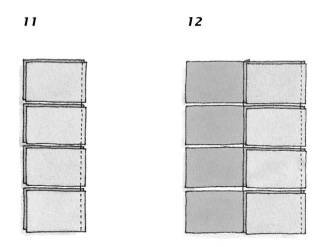

When machine piecing, the meeting of seams can, if tackled wrongly, become too bulky. Pressing instructions are given with individual projects; following these will ensure that the seams nest neatly together.

Taming seam crossings is necessary where seams meet in the middle of a pinwheel, otherwise they will form a nasty lump. If the seams all lie in the same direction, the lump goes. To enable the last seam stitched to lie similarly, unpick a few stitches within the seam allowance of the the two seams at right angles to it. Do this carefully, being sure not to unpick nearer the seam allowance than one stitch. Trim off any projecting triangle points and press.

Pressing is an important part of machine piecing, it must be done as you go along, and not left to the end, as is often the case with hand piecing.

Seams can be finger pressed first, this is when the seam is pushed over and squeezed between your thumb and finger. The work can then be pressed with an iron both on the wrong and the right side to ensure that no pleats are pressed in. Always press in the direction of the grain and not across the bias which will stretch the pieces.

ADDING BORDERS
Borders with butted edges

These borders are the easiest and quickest to stitch, and if this is your first quilt, they are probably preferable. Although some of the projects in the book give measurements for the borders, always check the measurements of your quilt top before cutting these long strips.

1 To determine the length of the side borders, measure centre top to centre bottom of the quilt. Cut two borders of this length by the required width.

2 Pin to the side edges, adjusting the quilt top to fit as necessary, then stitch using an exact ¼ in/0.75 cm seam allowance. Press the seam towards the border.

3 Once the side borders have been stitched, measure the work again, this time from centre side to centre side. This determines the length of the top and bottom borders. Cut two border strips this length.

4 Pin and stitch to the top and bottom edges of the quilt. Press towards the border. If more than one border is required, simply repeat the process.

Borders with mitred corners

These borders take a bit more time but give a professional finish to your quilt.

1 Determine the length and width of your quilt top by measuring from centre top to centre bottom and from centre side to centre side.

2 Cut border pieces to these measurements plus twice the width of the border plus approximately 2 in/5 cm extra for the seam allowance.

3 Pin a border strip to the quilt edge, matching the strip centre to the quilt edge centre. Allow the excess border fabric to extend beyond each end.

4 Stitch to the quilt edge using an exact ¼ in/0.75 cm seam allowance, starting and finishing ¼ in/0.75 cm from the corner (diagram 13).

13

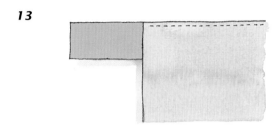

5 Repeat with the remaining borders. Press the seam allowances towards the borders.

6 To form the mitres, lay the quilt wrong side up, then either press the borders (diagram 14), match the folds, pin and stitch, finishing at the inner corner, or overlap the corners (diagram 15) and place the 45° line of your ruler on the raw edge of the border. Pencil a line from the border seam to the outside edge. Overlap the adjacent border and mark again.

14

15

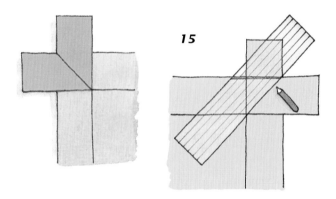

7 With right sides together, match the drawn lines, pin and stitch along the marked line (diagram 16).

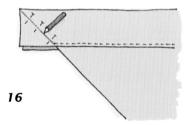

16

8 Check the right side, then trim to ¼ in/0.75 cm. Press this seam allowance open. Whichever method you choose, repeat on the remaining three corners.

QUILTING

The primary function of the quilting stitches is to hold the three layers of the quilt (top, wadding and backing) together securely enough to last the lifetime of the quilt. Traditional hand-quilting can be a slow process, therefore on the quilts featured in this book, the quilting is either by machine or there are suggestions for quick hand-quilting designs. You can always change from machine to hand-quilting if time is not a factor.

Marking quilting designs

Designs can be as complicated or as simple as you wish. If you intend to machine-quilt, look for designs that can be stitched in a continuous motion. Quick quilting designs make use of seam lines or the pattern on the fabric. Any other designs need to be marked before the quilt is layered.

There are a variety of marking tools available: 2H pencils, silver and yellow quilters' pencils, washable marking pens, etc. Whichever you choose, always test the marker on a scrap of the fabric you have used in your quilt, you should be able to remove your designs after you have quilted.

The quilt top then needs to be attached to the backing and wadding, by either bagging-out or layering.

Bagging-out

This is a quick method which neatens the edges of a quilt in place of adding a binding.

1 Lay the wadding out on a flat surface. Lay the backing fabric on top of the wadding, right side up, then lay the quilt top, right side down, on top.

2 Trim the backing fabric and the wadding to the same size as the quilt top all round. Take care not to cut into the quilt top when doing this.

3 Pin the layers together, then stitch round the edges, leaving a gap long enough to turn the quilt through (diagram 17).

17

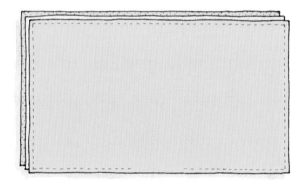

4 Trim the wadding close to the seam line, then turn the quilt through, so that the wadding is in the centre of the sandwich. Close the opening with small invisible ladder stitches.

5 Baste with thread or safety pins ready for quilting as described below.

Layering
The backing and wadding should be slightly bigger all round than the quilt top.

1 Lay out the backing fabric right side down, smooth out and stretch taut. If possible, stick the edge at intervals with masking tape. Lay the wadding on the top of the backing and the quilt top on the top of the wadding with right side up.

2 Pin the layers together starting from the centre and working out, keeping the fabrics smooth.

Basting
This is necessary to hold the three layers securely together all over the quilt, so that the fabrics don't wrinkle when quilted. It can be done with thread or safety pins.

1 When using thread, take long pieces of thread, start in the middle and baste out to the edge in rows in both directions (diagram 18).

18

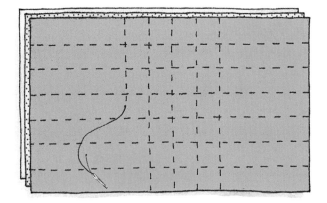

2 When using safety pins, these should be placed all over the quilt at intervals no greater than a hand's width in any one direction. Use short, fine and rustless pins to avoid permanently marking the quilt.

3 Short plastic tags are now available that can be shot through the quilt with a basting gun instead of using safety pins.

Machine-quilting
When a quilt is machine-quilted, a continuous line of thread is visible on both the top and the back of the quilt; you need, therefore, to choose a lightweight thread to work with. Threads are numbered in such a way that the lighter the thread, the higher the number. Before quilting your project, make up a sample sandwich of backing, wadding and top fabrics as used in the quilt and try different threads to achieve the effect that you like. You can even choose an invisible thread if you wish.

Needles are numbered 70/10, 80/12, 90/14, etc. The finer the needle, the lower the number: 70/10 or 80/12 are suitable for both piecing and quilting with lightweight or invisible thread.

A walking or even-feed foot is essential to prevent tucks forming in the quilt top or backing. This foot is used with the feed dogs up and therefore is the best technique for designs with continuous, fairly straight lines. You can turn wide curves and pivot but you cannot turn tight curves. It is used for stitching in-the-ditch, simple outline stitching and stitching in a grid design. For tight curves or freehand quilting, you will need to use the darning foot with the feed dogs down.

When you are using a walking or even-feed foot, the machine controls the direction and the stitch length. In general, the stitch length needs to be longer than for regular stitching. To start and end a line of quilting, set the stitch length to very short and stitch about eight stitches, then snip off the loose threads close to the surface of the quilt.

In-the-ditch
One of the simplest, and therefore most popular, methods of machine-quilting is quilting in-the-ditch. When a top is pieced and pressed all the seams have a low side with no seam allowance underneath: this is the ditch. The quilting is done on this side close to the seam.

Freehand quilting
With this method you control the direction and the length of the stitches by moving the quilt forwards, backwards and sideways under the needle of the sewing machine. You will need much practice to achieve perfect results.

Hand-quilting
To hand-quilt you need to select a stronger thread than that used for normal stitching. There are several makes of quilting thread on the market. Choose a colour of quilting thread that will either blend or contrast with the fabrics for the top and backing; the choice is yours. If you wish, you can use different colours in the same quilt. Special needles called "betweens" are used and you need to select a 9, 10 or 12. The larger the number, the smaller the needle. The quilt top needs to be held flat either in a frame or in a hoop.

Frame

Some floor frames do not require the quilt to be basted; the layers are held together by the frame.

1 Baste the backing fabric, wrong side up, to the tape that is fixed to the front and back rollers of the frame. Roll the excess backing fabric onto the back roller until the fabric in the frame is taut.

2 Attach the bottom edge of the wadding to the backing fabric along the front roller only, using long basting stitches. Smooth the wadding towards the back of the frame.

3 Arrange the quilt top over the wadding; baste through all three layers along the front edge only.

4 To hold the wadding and quilt top in position along the far edge of the frame, use long, fine pins or needles. The wadding and quilt top hang loose over the back roller.

5 Quilt the area in front of you, then release the tension and roll more backing off the back roller. Wind the quilted part onto the front roller, re-tension and continue to quilt.

Hoop

Hoops can be hand-held (round and oval) or on a floor stand. If you are using a hand-held hoop, choose a 14 in/35 cm or 16 in/40 cm diameter for ease. Hoops on floor stands can have a bigger diameter. Hoops are considered to be more portable and they allow you to turn the work. Do not leave a quilt in a hoop when you are not working on it, as this will distort your piece.

Layer and baste the quilt, then place the quilt over the bottom ring and place the top ring over the quilt. Tighten the ring: the fabric need not be as tight as a drum skin, but the work should be smooth. Work from the centre outwards.

Simple scroll frames are also available which will allow you the portability of a hoop while working with a frame.

The quilting process

The goal in hand-quilting is to form straight, even stitches with the same size space in between as the length of thread showing.

1 Cut a length of thread about 18 in/45 cm long and tie a single knot in the end cut from the spool.

2 To start quilting, enter the work with a flat knot about ¾ in/ 2 cm from where you want to start quilting, run the needle through the wadding only and come up at the starting point. Pull the thread sharply and the knot will "pop" through the surface and lodge in the wadding.

3 To quilt, the needle needs to enter the fabric at a perpendicular angle. Hold the needle between your thumb and forefinger and place the point where you wish to form the first stitch. Push the needle through the quilt, so that it only just pierces the under surface, then lodge the eye of the needle in the end of your thimble. The end of your forefinger under the quilt will just feel the tip of the needle. Some quilters like to wear a second thimble or some other protection on the finger of their underneath hand.

4 The underneath finger pushes upwards at the same time as the thimble rocks the eye end of the needle towards the surface of the quilt. The point of the needle will reappear through the top.

5 Rock the needle with the thimble into a perpendicular position and re-enter the fabric.

6 Repeat until you have a few stitches on the needle. Pull the thread through and repeat the process (diagram 19).

19

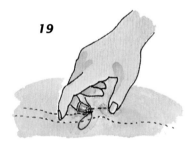

7 To finish off, quilt until you have about 6 in/15 cm of thread left, then make a knot by passing the needle round the thread to form a loop and passing the needle through the loop. Pull the loop to the surface of the quilt and tighten to form a knot. Take one more stitch and "pop" the knot through the surface. Take the needle through the wadding and back through the surface of the quilt, pull the thread taut, then cut off close to the surface.

TYING A QUILT

A quick alternative to quilting is tying. By this method the top, wadding and backing sandwich is held together by a grid of knots stitched through all three layers. The thread for this needs to be thicker: coton perlé is good or double knitting wool for a rustic effect – details are given with individual quilt instructions. A sharp needle with a large eye is essential. Use a long length of thread to allow for multiple tying.

1 Starting in the centre of the place where you wish to position the tie, take a stitch through all three layers, draw the thread through, leaving a tail about 6 in/15 cm long. Re-enter the quilt at the point where the next tie is to be and take another stitch, leaving a loop between stitches.

2 Repeat, without cutting, until there is a stitch in each of the places to have a tie (diagram 20).

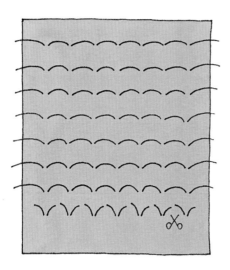

3 Cut between the stitches, then tie the threads using a surgeon's square knot (diagram 21).

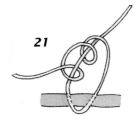

BINDING THE QUILT

If the quilt has been bagged-out, it will not need a binding. Otherwise, after quilting, trim the edges, so that all three layers are level. The binding is best done with doublefold binding which can be cut either straight or on the bias. This can be made from straight strips joined together or as a continuous bias strip.

Continuous strip bias binding

1 Cut a square and mark the edges **A**, **B**, **C** and **D**; cut through the diagonal (diagram 22), then stitch **A** to **B** with a ¼ in/0.75 cm seam allowance (diagram 23).

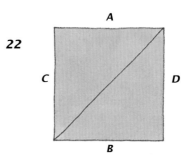

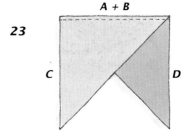

2 Open out and press the seam open. Draw lines the width of the bias you are making on the wrong side of the fabric (diagram 24).

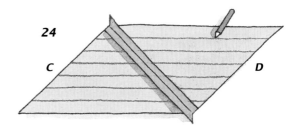

3 Make a tube by joining **C** to **D**, right sides together, but dropping the seam by one strip and matching the marked lines. Pin and stitch the seam (diagram 25). Press open.

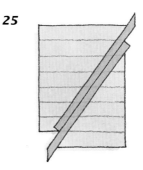

4 Cut the tube open along the marked lines in a continuous line (diagram 26).

26

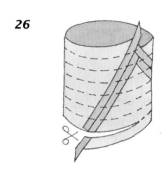

Doublefold binding

1 Fold the fabric strip in half lengthwise, right side out, and press lightly.

2 Starting somewhere along one edge of the quilt, start to pin the binding to the quilt, leaving a tail (diagram 27).

27

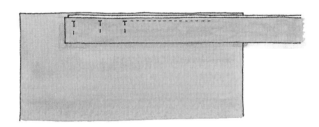

3 Stitch, using ¼ in/0.75 cm seam allowance, until you are ¼ in/0.75 cm from the corner. Reverse stitch and break off the thread.

4 Fold the binding away from the quilt at a right angle (diagram 28), then fold it back down on itself, matching the edge of the binding with the edge of the quilt (diagram 29).

28   **29**

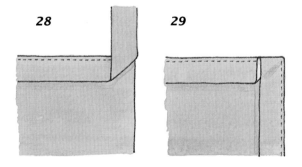

5 Starting ¼ in/0.75 cm from the corner, stitch to the next corner and repeat. Continue in this way until you are back where you started.

6 Fold back the two ends (diagram 30). Finger press, then stitch together along the creases. Trim back to ¼ in/0.75 cm.

30

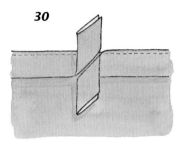

7 Turn the binding over the edge to the back of the quilt, slip stitch down covering the machine stitches. At the corners, mitres will fall on both front and back.

ADDING A HANGING SLEEVE

If your quilt is to be hung, either on the wall at home or in an exhibition, it will need a hanging sleeve.

1 Cut a piece of fabric 9 in/23 cm wide and to the length of the quilt. Turn a ½ in/1 cm hem at each short end and machine stitch.

2 Fold in half along its length, right sides together, and stitch the raw edges together with a ½ in/1 cm seam. Turn right sides out and press, so that the seam is in the middle. You can adjust the pressing of the sleeve at this point, so that the front of the sleeve is deeper than the back. When stitched to the quilt, the sleeve will have a slight bulge which will accommodate the thickness of the hanging pole.

3 Slipstitch the sleeve to the back of the quilt along the top and bottom edges, placing the top edge just below the binding and making sure that the seam side is underneath.

LABELLING A QUILT

It is important to sign and date your quilt as a record for yourself and future generations. The label you stitch onto your quilt can be simple or elaborate. There are books of scrolls that you can trace onto a simple calico label with a fine permanent pen. You can iron freezer paper to the wrong side of the label and type the details on the fabric. Remove the freezer paper before stitching the label to the reverse of the quilt.

ZIGZAGS and MEANDERS

The first two of my country quilts are based on ancient patterns, adapted to be made from appliqué or strips, then laid out in a quite formal "strippy style". The next three quilts are made from the same combination of strip widths in twists on traditional patterns, so that two come out with zigzags and another as a large weave. The sixth quilt is an unusual star pattern. I can imagine them as a splash of cheerful colour in a white-washed beamy attic bedroom on a brass or solid wood bedstead.

My fabrics for the first five are not scraps, because working with these usually takes longer. Like me, you will probably find that the choice of one fabric leads inevitably in a certain direction to the second and third – sometimes with unexpected results!

For speed you need to use the rotary cutter and sewing machine. For relaxation, you might choose to hand-piece (not me!) or hand-quilt. Whatever methods you use, the initial choices of design and colour will take just the same time. Why not take advantage of preplanning, and try a ready-designed quilt?

— PAULINE ADAMS

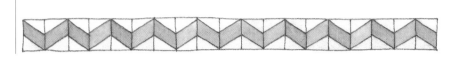

GREEK KEY PATTERN

This ancient pattern, often found on early Greek pottery in black and terracotta, is still a popular design motif in its many (some very complicated) variations. I originally designed this for strip piecing but found an irresistible dress fabric which would have been hard to piece because of its stretchy weave and linear pattern. So the design evolved to a true counterchange pattern in appliqué. It took approximately eight hours. This size of quilt will make a jazzy topper for a single bed or an eye-catching sofa throw.

Quilt size: 66 x 54 in/165 x 135 cm

MATERIALS

All fabrics used in the quilt top are 45 in/115 cm wide.

Black, fine-point, permanent marker pen
Tracing or greaseproof paper
Fusible webbing: 18 x 27 in/45.5 x 70 cm
Charcoal grey print fabric: 1¾ yards/1.6 metres
Cinnamon plain fabric: 1¾ yards/1.6 metres

Baking parchment paper
Cinnamon rayon machine embroidery thread
Card
Wadding: 2 oz polyester, 70 x 58 in/175 x145 cm
Backing: calico or sheeting, 70 x 58 in/175 x 145 cm
Clear nylon machine-quilting thread

ALTERNATIVE COLOUR SCHEMES

Although this pattern uses only two fabrics, it can look completely different, depending on which colours you choose to work with. Indigo and calico still provide a strong contrast but are more rural and folksy; blue and green prints are close together on the colour wheel, producing a subtle and feminine look; splashy roses for the darker shade with a toning pastel pink look romantic and cottagey and a homespun type check with a strong contrast plain makes a very popular combination.

❝When choosing large-scale prints to use in large areas, as in this pattern, be sure to preview a good expanse of the fabric to ensure its suitability.❞

21

CUTTING

1 Draw the cutting pattern (diagram 1) for the key appliqué pieces, using the lines on your cutting mat as a guide, a rotary ruler and permanent marker pen to enlarge the diagram, onto greaseproof or tracing paper. Lay the fusible webbing on top of the pattern (paper side up) and trace the pattern twice onto the paper backing.

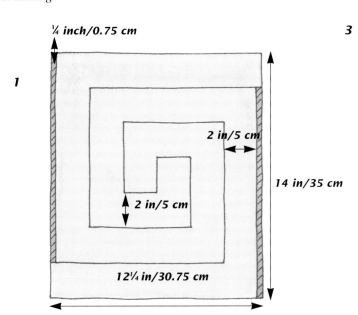

2 From the charcoal print, cut lengthwise pieces (diagram 2). Cut one **A** strip, 28½ x 56½ in/71.5 x 141.5 cm; one **C** strip, 5 ½ in x 56½ in/14 x 141.5 cm; and one full length strip 5½ in/14 cm wide, sub-cut into one **D** strip, 28½ in/71.5 cm long; one **E** strip, 16½ in/41.5 cm long and two **F** squares, 5½ in/14 cm.

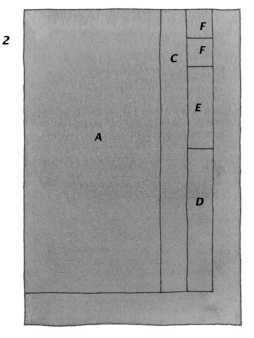

3 From the cinnamon plain fabric, cut lengthwise pieces (diagram 3). Cut one **B** strip, 16½ x 56½ in/ 41.5 x 141.5 cm; one **C**, one **D** and one **E** strip, and two **F** squares as for the charcoal print.

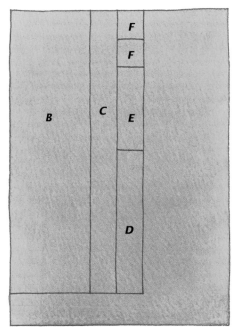

4 Following manufacturer's instructions with fusible webbing, iron the drawn patterns to the wrong side of the remaining cinnamon fabric, ensuring lines are on grain. Use baking parchment paper between fusible webbing and iron to protect the surfaces.

5 Carefully cut (with scissors) along all the drawn lines. Discard the four very narrow slivers, and you will have four square-spiral key pieces.

STITCHING

All seam allowances are a scant ¼ in/0.75 cm.

1 Using the quilt plan, lay the key pieces in place on the right side of charcoal piece **A**, noting that the top key is spaced a seam's width from the top edge, and all the rest 2 in/5 cm apart. The tails are all flush with the long raw side edge of **A**. Adjust positions before peeling off the protective paper backing from one key, replacing it and ironing it in position, using the baking parchment paper for protection again. Repeat with the remaining three shapes.

2 With cinnamon thread, stitch the key shapes down, close to their edges. This stitching will be hidden later.

3 Pin and stitch **A** to **B**, catching the ends of the key shapes into the seam.

ADDING THE BORDERS

1 Pin the long borders, **C**, to the sides of the quilt top. Press all seams towards charcoal fabric.

2 Pin and stitch a border strip **D** to **E**, short ends together and repeat, reversing the colour sequence (see quilt plan) to make two short border strips. Add a small **F** square on either end, then pin and stitch these to the top and bottom of the quilt, matching seam lines. Press all seams towards charcoal fabric.

FINISHING THE QUILT

1 Paste the paper key pattern onto card. Cut out the spirals. Place the patterns in position on the quilt top (diagram 4) and mark round them. Note that tails of the pattern do not reach the appliqué – just extend lines with a ruler. Repeat down the length of the quilt.

4

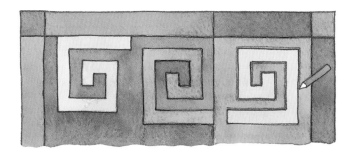

2 Lay out the wadding. Place the patchwork centrally on top, right side up, and safety-pin the layers together.

3 With cinnamon embroidery thread through the machine needle, loosen thread tension slightly, and set machine for a wide zigzag, with a very short stitch length. Practise first on some spare fabric and wadding. Zigzag the quilt all round the key shapes, just covering their raw edges. If you want consistency, zigzag all round the other cinnamon pieces also, but not round any outside edges.

4 Trim the wadding to the size of the quilt top. Lay out the backing, right side up, and lay quilt top centrally on it, right sides together. Pin around edges, and stitch all round ¼ in/ 0.75 cm from the edge, leaving a gap large enough to turn the quilt through.

5 Trim the corners and excess backing. Turn through and close the gap by hand. Safety-pin again through all layers.

6 With clear nylon thread through the needle, machine-quilt on all seamlines and on the marked key shapes.

❝When quilting the key shapes, stitch all the lengthwise lines first, then the crosswise ones, rather than trying to quilt a continuous line round all the key corners.❞

BLUE MEANDERS

This is another ancient, very graphic pattern. Here I have set it in an unorthodox way as a strippy, running from top to bottom for a single bed quilt. It will take roughly 20 hours.

◆

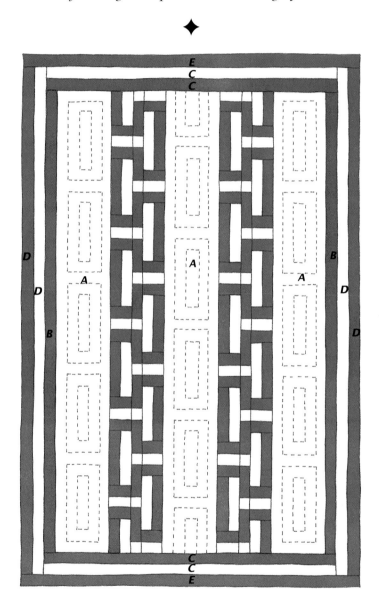

Quilt size: 94 x 62 in/235 x 155 cm

MATERIALS

All fabrics used in the quilt top are 45 in/115 cm wide.

White fabric: 4 yards/3.7 metres
Dark blue print fabric: 1½ yards/1.4 metres

Backing: calico or sheeting, 70 x 99 in /178 x 250 cm
Wadding: 2 oz polyester, a single bed-sized piece
Quilting thread: 2 skeins blue coton perlé no. 5 (optional)

CUTTING

1 Refer to the quilt plan and from the white fabric, cut (lengthwise) three background **A** strips 10½ in x 94 in/ 26.5 x 235 cm long, two **D** strips 2½ in x 94 in/6.5 x 235 cm and two **C** strips 2½ x 58 in/6.5 x 146.5 cm. Reserve for trimming to length later.

2 From the remaining white fabric, cut 11 crosswise strips, 2½ in/6.5 cm wide.

3 From the blue fabric, cut two crosswise strips, 6½ in/ 16.5 cm wide and 26 crosswise strips 2½ in/6.5 cm wide. Reserve 15 of these strips for the borders.

STITCHING

The blue and white strips must be stitched into three different strip arrangements as shown in diagram 1 before pressing and cutting pattern units. Press all the strips towards the blue fabric.

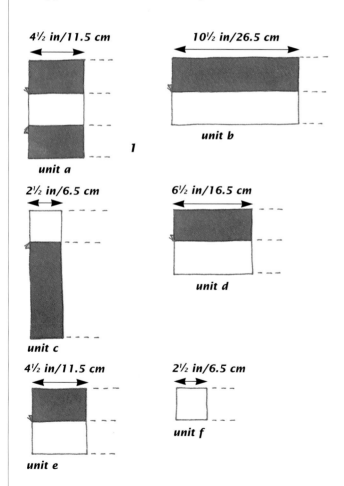

4½ in/11.5 cm

10½ in/26.5 cm

unit b

1

unit a

2½ in/6.5 cm

6½ in/16.5 cm

unit d

unit c

4½ in/11.5 cm

2½ in/6.5 cm

unit f

unit e

1 For **a** units, you will need two lengths of a sandwich of two narrow blue strips stitched to one narrow white strip. Cut across into 18 lengths of 4½ in/11.5 cm.

2 For **c** units, you will need two lengths of one narrow white strip stitched to one 6½ in/16.5 cm wide blue strip. Cut across into 20 slices, each 2½ in/6.5 cm wide.

2

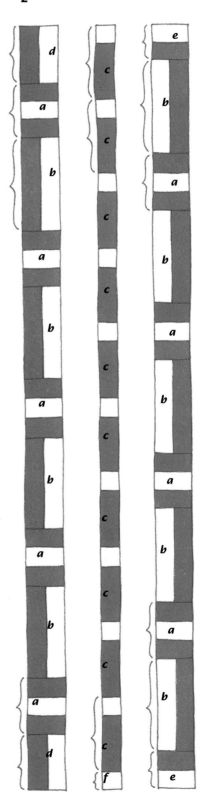

3 For the remaining units you will need eight lengths of one narrow white strip stitched to one narrow blue strip. From these, first cut 18 **b** units, $10^{1}/_{2}$ in/26.5 cm long. Next cut four **d** units $6^{1}/_{2}$ in/16.5 cm long; four **e** units $4^{1}/_{2}$ in/11.5 cm long and two white **f** units, $2^{1}/_{2}$ in/6.5 cm square. (For the latter, unpick a seam from the left-over joined strips if necessary.)

4 Divide the units into two equal piles and work first with one of them. Following diagram 2 on page 26, start at the top of the left-hand strip and work downwards. Stitch the top **d** unit to an **a** unit, adding alternate **b** and **a** units until you have used five **a** units; finish with the second **d** unit.

5 For the middle strip, stitch 10 **c** units end to end, and finish with a white **f** square.

6 For the right-hand strip, start at the top with an **e** unit stitched to a **b** unit, then alternate **a** and **b** units until all have been used up, finishing with the final **e** unit.

7 Press all the strips, then pin and stitch the lengths together following diagram 2. Press again. Make the second patchwork strip exactly the same.

ASSEMBLY AND BORDERS

1 Stitch the reserved blue strips into one long length. Press the seams open. Measure the length of the patchwork pattern strips and cut the three reserved wide white background pieces (**A**) to this length.

2 Cut two lengths off the blue stripping to the same measurement (border strips **B**).

3 For border strips **D**, cut two lengths of blue stripping and two of white all 8 in/20 cm longer than **A** and **B**. Reserve.

4 Assemble the top, including borders **B**, noting that the right-hand patchwork strip must be turned end-to-end to mirror the left-hand strip. Pin, stitch and press all long seams.

5 Measure across the patchwork centre side to centre side; cut two white and two blue **C** border strips to this length, and two blue **E** border strips 8 in/20 cm longer. Pin and stitch blue and white pairs of border strips together. Press the seams towards the blue borders.

6 Pin and stitch the border strips to the patchwork, first **C** strips to top and bottom, then **D** strips to each side and finally **E** strips to top and bottom. Press the seams towards the blue fabric between additions.

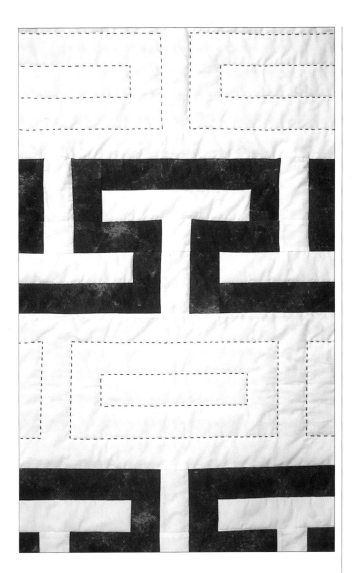

FINISHING THE QUILT

1 Using the patchwork as a guide, lightly mark the horizontal lines for the rectangles in the plain strips, then mark the vertical lines, which are 2 in/5 cm apart.

2 Layer the backing, wadding and patchwork. Safety-pin through all the layers.

3 Machine-quilt in-the-ditch around the patchwork patterns and on all the border seams (except the crosswise joining seams). Machine-quilt in the white background strips or sashiko quilt the pattern, using coton perlé in a matching blue.

4 Trim the wadding $^{1}/_{4}$ in/0.75 cm smaller than the quilt top. Trim the backing to the same size as the quilt top. Turn the backing in to enclose the wadding and turn the top in to match, both with $^{1}/_{4}$ in/0.75 cm turnings. Pin and machine stitch all round, close to the edge.

RAIL FENCE VARIATION

This quilt pattern is based on the traditional American pattern "Rail Fence", but I have changed the strips from equal to varied width and changed the set of the patchwork blocks to on point. Using one wide strip eliminates seams and so is quicker. These changes result in an unusual zigzag effect design.

The fabrics chosen are strong and bright. The wider print strip counterbalances the narrower blue. It took about twelve hours to make, and is sized for a child's bed, a throw, a lap quilt or even a topper for a double bed.

Quilt size: 57 x 57 in/143 x 143 cm

MATERIALS

All fabrics used in the quilt top are 45 in/115 cm wide.

Printed fabric for wide strips and outer border: 2⅛ yards/1.9 metres
White (or light) plain fabric for narrow strips: ⅞ yard/80 cm

Dark plain fabric for narrow strips and inner border: 1¼ yards/1.1 metres
Card
Backing: calico or sheeting, 60 in/155 cm square
Wadding: 2 oz polyester, 60 in/155 cm square
Double knitting yarn

CUTTING

1 From the printed fabric, cut 14 crosswise strips, 4½ in/ 11.5 cm wide. Reserve six for the outer border.

2 From the white fabric, cut eight crosswise strips, 2½ in/ 6.5 cm wide.

3 From the dark plain fabric, cut 13 crosswise strips, 2½ in/6.5 cm wide. Reserve five for the inner border.

STITCHING

1 Stitch the strips into sets of three using a scant ¼ in/ 0.75 cm seam allowance. Press the seams towards the print fabric (diagram 1).

1

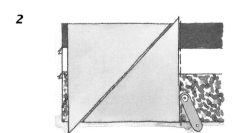

2 Measure across the stripping, and cut it into 24 squares of that measurement. This is most easily done with a large square rotary ruler, but may also be done with a card template cut to the right size and laid as a guide under an ordinary rotary ruler.

3 Make a triangular card template, with the short sides ³⁄₈ in/1.125 cm longer than the side of the squares you have just cut.

4 Cut 16 half-blocks for the quilt edges from the remaining stripping (diagram 2), noting that each half-block triangle will have one point missing. Pin and stitch the blocks and half-blocks in diagonal rows (diagram 3). Finger press the seams.

2

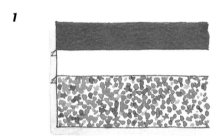

3

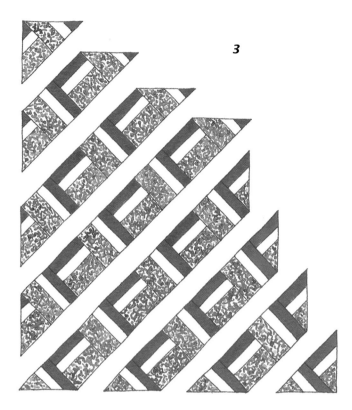

5 Stitch the rows together into a square. Finger press the seams. Tame the seam crossings. Press carefully on-grain so as not to distort the bias edges.

ADDING THE BORDERS

1 Stitch the five reserved dark plain fabric strips for the inner border into one long length. Press the seams open.

2 Measure the patchwork across the centre. Cut two dark strips to this length, and two strips 4 in/10 cm longer. Following the quilt plan, pin and stitch the two shorter borders to the opposite sides of the patchwork, then the two longer strips to the remaining sides. Press the seams outwards.

3 Stitch the six reserved printed fabric strips for the outer border into one long length. Press. Measure the patchwork across the centre again. Cut two print strips to this length and two strips 8 in/20 cm longer. Pin and stitch the two shorter borders to opposite sides of the patchwork. Press. Finally stitch the two longer strips to the remaining sides. Press.

FINISHING THE QUILT

The quilt is machine-quilted in two stages before and after being bagged-out.

1 Cut the backing and wadding 4 in/10 cm larger in each direction than the quilt top.

2 Lay out the wadding. Place the quilt top right side up on top of it. Safety-pin the layers together at the centre of each block, along the middle of the print border and in the triangular edge blocks.

3 Machine-quilt in-the-ditch on the long edges of all the white plain strips, and between the two border strips. If desired, also quilt along the centre of all the print strips in the blocks. Trim off any excess wadding.

4 Leaving the pins in, lay out the patchwork right side up. Lay the backing on top, right side down. Pin. Stitch around ¼ in/0.75 cm from the patchwork edge, but leave an opening about 12 in/30 cm long for turning the quilt through. Trim any excess backing and snip off the corners. Turn through. Close seam by hand.

5 Safety-pin again through all layers. Machine-quilt in-the-ditch round the individual blocks, the inner border seam and ½ in/1.5 cm from the outside edge.

6 If desired, tie through all the layers on the print strips and borders. The positions are marked on the quilt plan. Use double knitting yarn, doubled, and a large-eyed sharp needle. A quick, economical knot is shown in diagram 4. To do this, take a stitch through all layers, pull yarn through, leaving a 2 in/5 cm tail on top. Flip the yarn in a loop around the far side of the tail, then take hold of the tail with one hand while passing the needle up through the front of the loop with the other. Pull firmly on the needle and tail to close the knot close to the quilt's surface. Trim off the ends to 1 in/2.5 cm.

4

WEAVE PATTERN

The same set of one wide and two narrow strips can be used in many different ways, by changing the colours, the strip sequence and/or the arrangement of blocks. Here the strips have been arranged differently, and the blocks are in two different colourways, so that the overall effect is of a piece of weaving. Instead of machine-quilting down the centre strips, try equally speedy tying or leisurely hand-quilting. The plain colours chosen are of equal strength to emphasize the pattern. This took roughly 11 hours and makes a pretty lap or child's quilt.

Quilt size: 49¼ x 49¼ in/123x 123 cm

MATERIALS

All fabrics used in the quilt top are 45 in/115 cm wide.

Pink cotton fabric: 1¼ yards/1.2 metres
Blue cotton fabric: 1 yard/90 cm
Calico: 1½ yards/1.4 metres

Card: about 10 in/25 cm square
Wadding: 2 oz polyester, 54 in/140 cm square
Clear nylon machine-quilting thread
Backing: calico or sheeting, 54 in/140 cm square

CUTTING

1 From the pink fabric, cut 15 crosswise strips, 2½ in/6.5 cm wide. Reserve five for the border.

2 From the blue fabric, cut 10 crosswise strips, 2½ in/6.5 cm wide.

3 From the calico, cut 10 crosswise strips, 4½ in/11.5 cm wide.

STITCHING

Use a scant ¼ in/0.75 cm seam allowance throughout.

1 Stitch the strips into ten sets of three – five of blue strips on either side of the calico and five of pink strips on either side of the calico (diagram 1). Press the seams away from the calico.

1

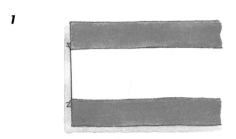

2 Measure across a pressed strip set. Cut 12 squares of each colourway of stripping to this measurement.

3 Cut a right-angled triangle template from the card, with short sides ½ in/1.25 cm longer than the measured stripping width. From the remaining stripping, cut eight triangle blocks of each colourway (diagram 2). Note that each half-block triangle will have one point missing.

2

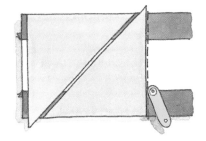

4 Following the quilt plan, lay out the blocks in pattern. Pin and stitch them together in diagonal strips (diagram 3). Press carefully so as not to distort the bias edges.

3

ADDING THE BORDERS

1 Stitch the reserved pink strips for the border into one long length. Press the seams open.

2 Measure across the centre of the quilt top. Cut two pieces to this measurement and two pieces 4 in/10 cm longer.

3 Pin on, then stitch the two shorter borders to opposite sides of the quilt top. Pin, then stitch the longer borders to the other two sides. Press.

FINISHING THE QUILT

The quilt is partly machine-quilted before being bagged-out, then machine-quilted again.

1 Mark a line for quilting down the centre of all the blocks, through the length of the calico strips.

2 Lay out the wadding. Lay the quilt top on top of the wadding, right side up and safety-pin the layers together.

3 Using nylon quilting thread through the machine needle and with a slightly lengthened stitch, machine-quilt in-the-ditch on the long edges of all the calico strips and on the marked lines. Trim the wadding to the size of the quilt top.

4 Lay out the backing, right side up. Lay the quilt top centrally on top of the backing, right side down. Pin around the edges. Stitch around the edge, ¼ in/0.75 cm in from the quilt edge, leaving a gap for turning through. Trim the corners. Turn through and close the gap by hand.

5 Safety-pin again. Machine-quilt ½ in/1.5 cm from the quilt edge, then in-the-ditch of the borders; finally machine-quilt in long diagonal lines across the quilt on all the block edges.

PUSS-IN-LIGHTNING

The traditional strippy quilt layout has wide alternate-coloured strips of fabric running the length of the quilt. I have used the "Puss in the Corner" block on point in vertical rows, but eliminated strip seams by setting it staggered and diagonally, like the other pattern "Streak of Lightning" – less stitching and more effect! The finish is machine-quilting, but you could embellish with ties or buttons. There will be one spare block, which could be used for a matching cushion. This size of quilt is suitable for a nap quilt or a throw and took about 12 hours.

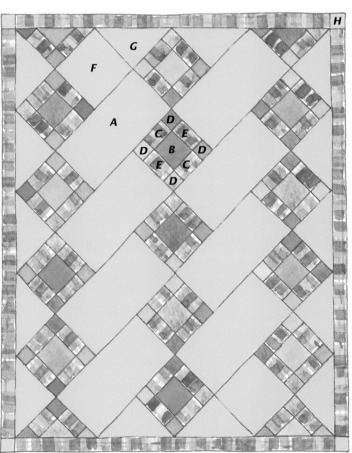

Quilt size: 60½ x 49¼ in/154.5 x 123 cm

MATERIALS

All fabrics used in the top are 45 in/115 cm wide.

Background fabric: plain colour, 1¾ yards/1.5 metres
Checked fabric: 1½ yards/1.3 metres
Plain fabric: six fat quarters in assorted colours

Wadding: 2 oz polyester, 65 in x 53 in/162 x 133 cm
Clear nylon machine-quilting thread
Backing: light-coloured calico or sheeting, 65 in x 53 in/162 x 133 cm

CUTTING

1 From the background fabric, cut four crosswise strips 8½ in/21.5 cm wide, then cut these into eight **A** pieces 16½ in/41.75 cm long and two **F** squares (see quilt plan).

2 From the same fabric, cut two crosswise strips 9 in/23 cm wide, and cut into seven squares. Cut these in half diagonally to make 14 **G** triangles.

3 From the background remnants, cut four **H** pieces 2½ in/5.5 cm square.

4 From the checked fabric, cut six crosswise strips 4½ in/11.5 cm wide, then cut in half.

5 Cut 11 crosswise strips 2½ in/6.5 cm wide, cut six of these in half and reserve the remaining five for the borders.

6 From each plain fabric fat quarter, cutting at right angles to the selvage, cut one strip 4½ in/11.5 cm wide and two strips 2½ in/6.5 cm wide.

STITCHING

All seams are a scant ¼ in/0.75 cm. For the blocks, the checked and plain fabric strips are stitched into sets of three, then re-cut and stitched into squares.

1 For the **B** and **C** pieces, start by stitching a narrow checked strip to each side of a wide plain strip; press seam allowances towards the check; trim the ends even and cut each of the six sets across into three lengths of 4½ in/11.5 cm (diagram 1).

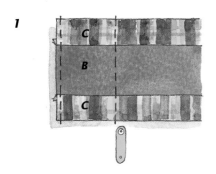

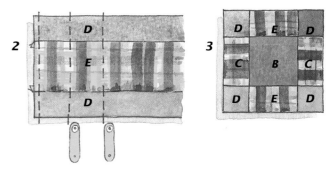

3 Lay out all these slices to form 18 blocks, making sure that each block contains five differently coloured plains (diagram 3). Pin and stitch the slices into blocks and press.

4 Lay out the quilt top as shown in diagram 4. Note that there will be one spare block, and that the four blocks sticking out at top and bottom will be trimmed later. Pin and stitch each row separately. Finger-press the seams away from the blocks.

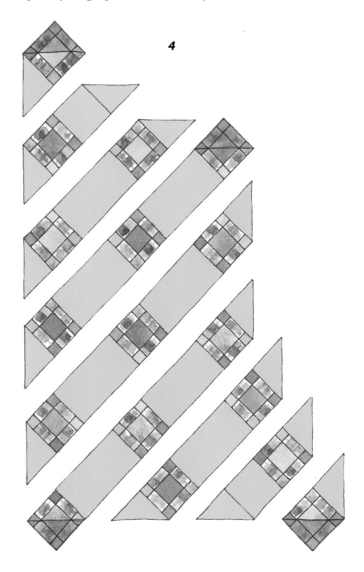

2 For **D** and **E** pieces, stitch one narrow plain strip on each side of a wide checked strip, making sure that the plains are different colours. Stitch into six sets; press the seams towards the check, trim the ends, then cut across into six slices 2½ in/6.5 cm wide (diagram 2).

5 Pin and stitch the diagonal rows together. Press carefully on grain so as not to distort the bias edges.

6 Using a rotary ruler, mark a line ¼ in/0.75 cm outside the block corners at the quilt top edges. Trim on this line.

ADDING THE BORDERS

1 For the border, stitch the reserved check strips together into one long length. Press the seams open.

2 Measure the quilt top width and length, through the centre. Cut two border strips to the measured width and two to the measured length. Pin on and stitch the short borders to the top and bottom of the quilt. Finger-press at the ends. Stitch one **H** square to each end of the two long border strips. Pin and stitch these strips to opposite sides. Press.

FINISHING THE QUILT

The quilt is machine-quilted in two stages – before and after bagging-out.

1 Mark the quilt top for quilting: using the rotary ruler, mark parallel zigzag lines to the blocks on the background fabric, spaced 2 in/5 cm away from them, with a third line halfway between.

2 Lay out the wadding smoothly, and place the quilt top on top, right side up, ensuring that the wadding is larger on all sides than the top. Safety-pin in all the block squares, along the border and on the background.

3 Machine-quilt with a lengthened stitch and clear nylon quilting thread. First stitch on all the marked zigzag lines, then in-the-ditch of the internal seamlines of the blocks.

4 Trim the excess wadding, so that it is the same size as the quilt top. Lay out the backing, right side up and lay the quilt top onto it, right side down. Pin all round, then stitch ¼ in/0.75 cm inside the edge of the quilt top, leaving a gap on one side large enough to turn the quilt through. Trim off the excess backing and clip the corners. Turn through.

5 Turn in and pin the seam allowances of the gap, and hand hem. Safety-pin again along the border and on all small corner squares of the blocks. Machine-quilt ¼ in/0.75 cm from outside edge, and in-the-ditch of the border and the block edges.

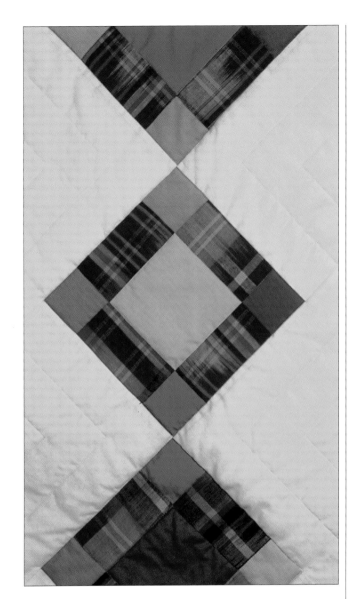

❝❝The use of a walking or even-feed foot is very helpful when machine-quilting. It feeds top and bottom fabrics through the machine evenly.❞❞

KIPPER STAR

This pattern gets its name from the four kipper-tie shapes which go to make up one star block. Alternative traditional American names are "Mountain Star" and "Stars and Stripes". By arranging the kipper units differently, a different star can be formed.

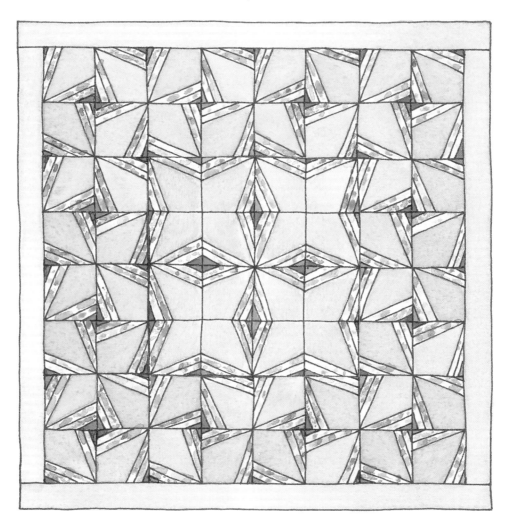

Quilt size: 54½ x 54½ in/136.5 x 136.5 cm

MATERIALS

All fabrics used in the quilt top are 45 in/115 cm wide.

Card or template plastic
Border fabric and square for wedges: plain cotton fabric, 3 yards/2.7 metres

Spray starch
Stripping: printed cotton fabric, 9 assorted fat quarters
Backing: calico or sheeting, 60 x 60 in/ 1.5 x 1.5 metres
Wadding: 2 oz polyester, 60 x 60 in/1.5 x 1.5 metres

There are three different star formations in this quilt. I made it with pink poplin and floral cotton lawn scraps from my fabric hoard for the stripping, but the instructions assume new fabrics will be used. It can be made two ways. I made it by stitching the strips in turn onto a paper foundation square to which the central wedge had been pinned. A quicker way (taking about 14 hours) is to make stripping and stitch triangles of it onto the top of a square, then trim off the excess bits, which removes the tedious and messy stage of picking off the paper backing. The size of the quilt makes it suitable for a baby's cot, a knee quilt, or a nap quilt. You could try bright and zingy colours as an alternative to the pastels.

CUTTING

1 Cut a wedge-shaped template from card or template plastic (diagram 1 on page 45).

2 From the border/wedge fabric, cut the borders: two lengthwise strips, 3½ in/9 cm wide and 60 in/153 cm long and two more the same width but 66 in/168 cm long. These measurements are overlong to allow for variations in the finished size.

3 Spray-starch and press the remaining border/wedge fabric. From it cut 64 6½ in/16.5 cm squares. Place the wedge template on the right side of each square and mark both diagonal lines (diagram 2).

2

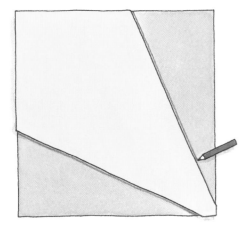

4 Divide the fat quarters for the stripping into three sets of three. Lay one set of three on the cutting mat. Trim the short sides and cut 1½ in/4 cm wide strips parallel to the short side, cutting a total of 11 strips. Repeat with the remaining two sets of three. There will be some remnants to use up on another project, or in case of accidents.

STITCHING

1 Stitch the strips together down the long sides in sets of three, varying the colour schemes as much as possible and using a scant ¼ in/scant 0.75 cm seam allowance. Press the seams to one side, then spray-starch and press again.

2 Trim across the end of each piece of stripping and cut across into two 8½ in/21.5 cm rectangles. Cut each rectangle in half diagonally. If you want your fabrics to be symmetrically placed around each wedge, be sure to cut the second rectangle of each set of stripping with the diagonal in the other direction (diagram 3). Cut 64 rectangles altogether.

3

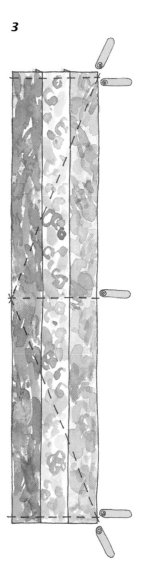

3 Pin and stitch a stripping triangle to a square, with the straight edge of the strip against the marked line (diagram 4). Remember to stitch with a scant seam allowance. Finger-press the stripping triangle outwards. Stitch a (matching) mirror-image triangle to the other side. Press, spray-starch and press again. It will be a strange shape until it is finally trimmed in step 4. Repeat step 3 until all the squares have had stripping triangles stitched to them.

4 Lay each pieced unit on the cutting mat, wrong side up. Use the square's edges as a guide to trim off excess stripping to make the unit 6½ in/16.5 cm square. Finally trim off the corner flaps of the square where they lie on the wrong side of the stripping.

4

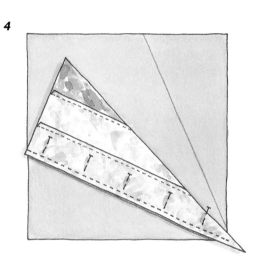

5 Place a large sheet on the floor and arrange the pieced units in sets of four to make stars (see quilt plan). Pin to the sheet to ensure that the arrangement does not get muddled. Remove the units from the sheet when you are ready to stitch them together, first into rows (finger-press seams open), then stitch the rows together (still finger-pressing the seams). Do not press with an iron until the borders are stitched on, otherwise all the bias edges will distort.

ADDING THE BORDERS

1 For the top and bottom borders, measure through the centre of the pieced top, centre side to centre side. Cut two border strips to this measurement. Pin and stitch on.

2 For the side borders, measure across the quilt, centre top to centre bottom and cut the remaining two border strips to fit. Pin and stitch them on. Press.

FINISHING THE QUILT

The quilt is bagged-out, then machine-quilted. You could tie it for a quicker finish or hand-quilt it at leisure.

1 Cut the backing exactly the same size as the completed top and the wadding 4 in/10 cm larger in each direction.

2 Mark the quilt top for quilting, if desired.

3 Lay the wadding out smoothly. Lay the pieced top over the wadding, right sides up, with the excess wadding extending evenly on all sides. Safety-pin the layers together. Lay the backing over the pieced top, right sides together and matching edges. Pin all round the edge. Turn over and trim the wadding evenly with the quilt top.

4 Stitch all round the quilt, ¼ in/0.75 cm in from the fabric edge but leave a gap of 8 in/20 cm in the centre of one side. Snip off corner points before turning through.

5 Re-pin through all the layers. Hand stitch the gap closed. Machine stitch all round the quilt ¼ in/0.75 cm from the edge. If you are machine-quilting, stitch around the kipper shapes, along all the block edges and in the border seams. Otherwise, tie through all three layers.

❝Take care not to stretch the bias edges of the quilt top when pinning and stitching the borders.❞

1

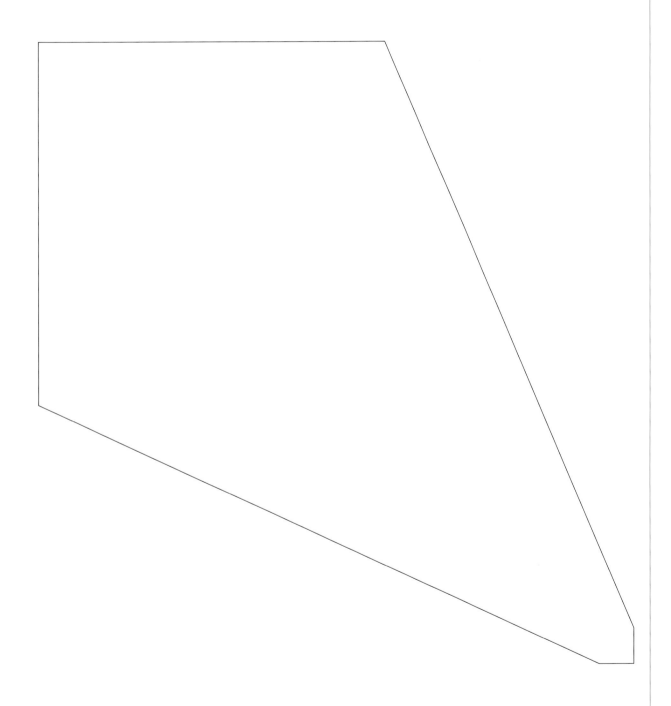

CHANGING SEASONS

The sewing machine, modern tools and the rotary cutter have revolutionized quiltmaking today; however, for me it is still important that we do not lose sight of the humble origins of the craft and this underlies my choice of fabrics and designs for the quilts in this chapter. I have incorporated modern techniques with traditional skills at the same time as using basic materials with simple block designs; I have taken a look at the ways in which these were used in the early days of quiltmaking.

Ideas for the quilt designs came mainly from old quilts; I took my colour inspiration from the countryside where I live and the ever-changing seasons.

— GILL TURLEY

BRACKEN

All the colours of bracken in autumn are contained in this lap quilt, ranging from the greens, burnished gold and bronze of the fronds to the muted browns of the woody stems. Soft, brushed-cotton fabrics, reminiscent of labourers' shirts of the past, are pieced to make the simple "Courthouse Steps" variation of the traditional "Log Cabin" block. It took about 24 hours. An interesting dimension is added to the overall design of this quilt by placing a large checked square between each log cabin block, which also speeds up the piecing. Utility quilting and buttons, of both leather and wood, add the final touches.

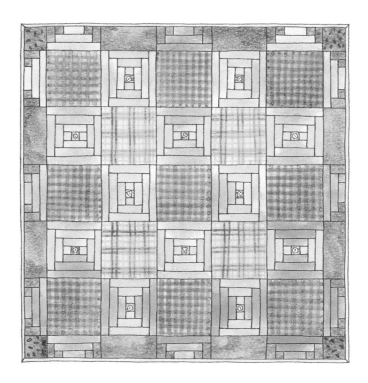

Quilt size: 59½ x 59½ in/151 x 151 cm

MATERIALS

All fabrics used in the quilt are 45 in/115 cm wide.

Small check fabric for the Courthouse Steps blocks: green, 50 in/125 cm; light gold, 40 in/100 cm
Big check fabric for Courthouse Steps small centre squares: dark green, 8 in/20 cm square
Big check fabric for large squares: dark green, 36 in/90 cm; light gold, l2 in/30 cm
Border blocks: dark brown small check, 20 x 45 in/ 50 x 115 cm

Corner squares for border: light brown small print, 12 in/15 cm square
Backing: 62 in/158 cm square
Wadding: cotton, 62 in/158 cm square ("Warm and Natural" is recommended)
Quilting thread: coton à broder or similar embroidery thread
Buttons: 12 assorted leather and wood buttons for tying
Binding: 24 in/60 cm square

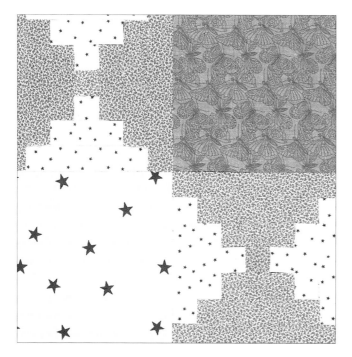 

ALTERNATIVE COLOUR SCHEMES

Different combinations of fabrics produce very different effects, particularly changing the relationship between the strips and the large squares. I have chosen four variations still with the country theme in mind. A combination of dark stars on a creamy background contrasted with clover pink produces a fresh look; dramatic stripes provide a strong accent amid soft purples and beiges; mossy greens and watery blues create an air of tranquility; while muted browns and blues combined with sand colours suggest fallow fields in winter.

COURTHOUSE STEPS BLOCKS
Cutting

1 Work on the small check fabrics for the strips and the big check for the small centre squares. From the green small check, cut one strip 5 x 26 in/13.5 x 66 cm (**a**). Keep this to use when making the "half" blocks for the border.

2 To cut the rest of the strips, place the green and light gold small check fabrics together. Cut across the full width of the fabric, cutting strips 2 in/5.5 cm wide.

3 From the dark green big check, cut twelve 2 in/5.5 cm squares for the centres of the blocks.

Stitching

1 Place a strip of light gold, check fabric under the machine foot and position the first centre square on top, right sides together. Line up the raw edges, then chain-piece, adding the squares until all twelve squares have been stitched. Press the seam towards the strip, then trim the blocks apart (diagram 1).

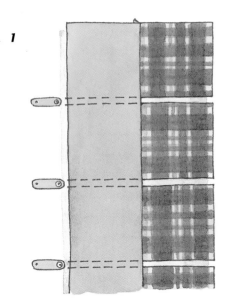

1

2 Stitch another light gold strip to the opposite side of the squares (diagram 2). Press and trim as before.

3 Chain-piece the green strips to the remaining two sides in the same way. Press and trim as before.

4 Continue adding the light gold and green rows until there are three rows on each side of the small squares. The twelve pieced blocks should each measure 11 in/33 cm square. However, if you are using more loosely woven cottons, these may be more stretchy, which could make a discrepancy in size.

2

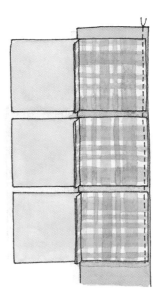

LARGE SQUARE BLOCKS
Cutting

1 Measure the 12 Courthouse Steps blocks and check that they are all the same size.

2 Cut out the big squares from the large check fabric. If the measurements are accurate, these will be cut as 11 in/33 cm squares. Cut four from the light gold and nine from the dark green. If your pieced blocks vary from the given measurement, then cut your large squares to match the size of your pieced blocks. Note that you will also need to adapt the measurements when making the "half" blocks for the border.

Stitching

1 Machine stitch the large squares to the Courthouse Steps blocks in rows (diagram 3), then join the rows together as in the sequence shown in the quilt plan. Press the seams towards the large squares.

3

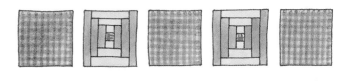

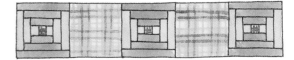

ADDING THE BORDERS

These are composed of "half" blocks, but without the row containing the centre square. If your Courthouse Steps blocks are accurately pieced, use the given measurements. If your finished block size differs, adjust the sizes for the following pieces accordingly.

Cutting

1 From the dark brown fabric, cut eight pieces 5 x 11 in/ 13.5 x 28.5 cm (**b**).

2 Cut the remaining dark brown fabric into 2 in/5.5 cm wide strips (**c**).

3 From the light brown fabric, cut four 5 in/13 cm squares for the border corners.

Stitching

1 To make the "half" blocks, machine stitch the dark brown **c** strips to each of the long edges of the green small check **a** piece. Press seams towards the dark brown strips.

2 Sub-cut every 2 in/5.5 cm to make the beginnings of the pieced "half" blocks, a total of 12 units (diagram 4).

4

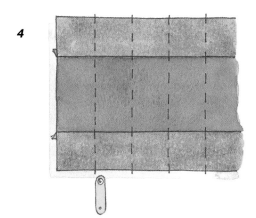

3 Stitch a long strip of green to one long side of these units. Press and trim.

4 Add dark brown **c** strips to each short side of the units. Press and trim.

5 Add one more green strip (diagram 5) to complete the "half" blocks.

5

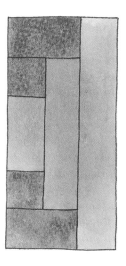

6 Alternating the blocks, join the "half" blocks to the **b** pieces, to make the four borders. To complete the top and bottom borders stitch a corner square to each end as in the quilt plan.

7 Stitch the short borders to opposite sides of the quilt top. Press the seams towards the borders.

8 Stitch the top and bottom borders to the remaining two edges of the quilt. Press the seams towards the borders.

FINISHING THE QUILT

1 Prepare the quilt for quilting. Layer the backing, wadding and quilt top. Baste the layers together.

2 Use thick thread and Utility Quilting (see page 63) to stitch diagonal lines from corner to corner on the plain blocks. In the centre of each pieced block, stitch a button. To finish, make a double bias binding and bind the quilt.

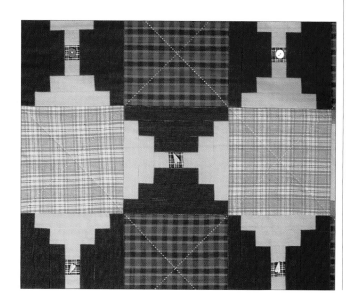

STRING PATCHWORK DIAMONDS

The string diamonds of this single bed quilt are made from shirting samples and are machine stitched onto diamond-shaped, calico foundation pieces. The striped fabrics used for the strings give a fan effect, achieved by stitching the strings at a slight angle, fanning from the centre outwards. A plain diamond is used to offset each string diamond. The quilt is finished with hand-quilting but for speed it could be machine-quilted or tied, when it will take about 30 hours. The layers on the foundation pieced diamonds add thickness and require no quilting.

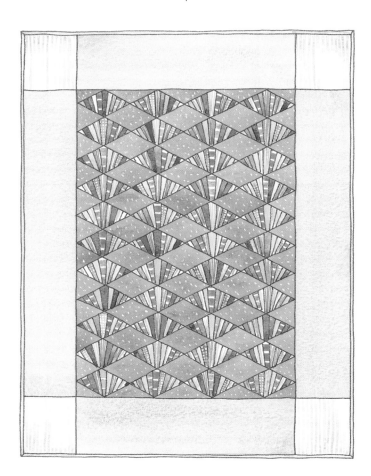

Quilt size: 54 x 58 in/138 x 148 cm

MATERIALS

All fabrics used in the quilt top are 45 in/115 cm wide.

Template plastic or thin card
For foundation diamonds: calico, 39 in/100 cm
For string diamonds: plenty of strips of scrap fabrics or 5 different fabrics, 12 in/30 cm of each

For plain diamonds: 39 in/100 cm
Border fabric: 39 in/100 cm
Corner squares fabric: 10 in/25 cm
Wadding: 60 x 72 in/152 x 183 cm
Backing: 60 x 72 in/152 x 183 cm
Binding: 24 in/60 cm square

String piecing was a popular way of making a quilt, either to recycle good pieces of cloth salvaged from old clothing or for using up odd pieces left over from dressmaking, these scraps were sometimes known as "strings". This method, which was formerly hand sewn with a running stitch, was known as "pick-up work". The bag of strings could be stored in readiness, the foundation shapes cut out and the work picked up and stitched, as and when time allowed. The diamond foundation shape could also be joined to make star blocks. Square and triangular foundations were popular, too, and used in other string patchwork designs.

CUTTING

1 Trace the diamond template (diagram 1 on page 57) onto the template plastic or thin paper which can then be stuck onto card. On your template mark the arrow to show the grain line, number each edge, then cut out the template carefully. Note that seam allowances are included. (Use the width from your sewing machine needle to the edge of the presser foot as the seam guide for all seams.)

2 To cut the foundation diamonds, position the template on the top left-hand corner of the calico, making sure that the arrow is in line with the straight grain of the calico. Position the ruler on top of the template and along edge **1** of the diamond. Make the first cut using the full length of the ruler (diagram 2). Before you move the ruler down to continue the cut, place a yard (metre) stick alongside, then carefully move the ruler along the edge of the stick and continue this first cut (diagram 3). Using the template as a width guide, place the ruler on top of the cut strip and parallel to the line you have just cut, then cut again along edge **2** of the diamond. (diagram 4). Repeat this process, cutting long strips.

> ❝ Use a piece of folded sticky tape to hold the template in position on the fabric. ❞

2

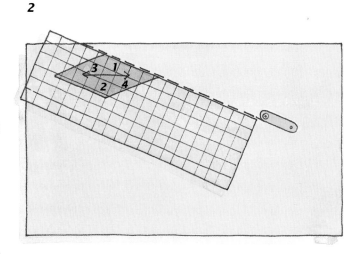

3

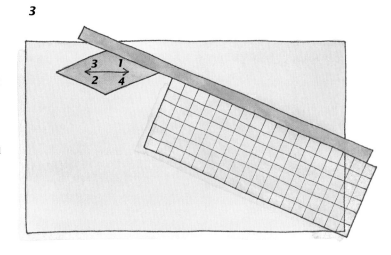

4

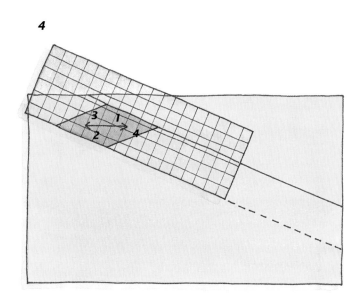

3 Layer the long rows carefully. Using the template as a guide, sub-cut the layered strips into diamonds using edges **3** and **4**. You will need a total of 44 diamonds (diagrams 5a and 5b).

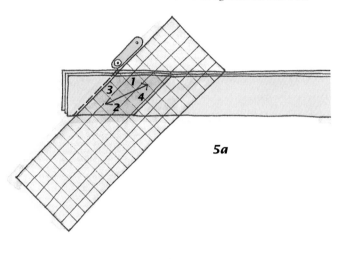

5a

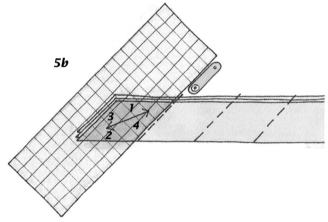

5b

4 Cut the scrap fabric into manageable pieces, roughly 1–1½ in/2.5–4 cm wide and long enough to reach from the tip to the base of the diamond foundation.

5 To cut the plain fabric diamonds, cut long strips as described in step 2, using the diamond template and long ruler. Do not sub-cut into diamonds.

STITCHING
Stitching strings to foundation diamonds

1 Position the first string right side up on top of the calico base (diagram 6). Take the next string, place it on top of the first string, right sides together, and move the bottom of this strip in a little, towards the centre (diagram 7). Machine stitch and flip the second string open. Finger press if you are using crisp cottons, but if you are using wool or other fabrics, these may need to be pressed with the steam iron.

6

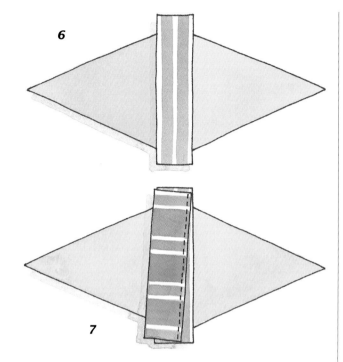

7

2 Continue stitching the strings in the same way to the left and right of the central strip, until the foundation is completely covered.

3 Excess bulk can be removed by trimming spare fabric from the seam allowance. Do not trim the strips level with the edges of the foundation until you have pressed the completed diamond with the iron. To hold the last strings firmly in place, I recommend machine top-stitching close to the edges of the diamond, at the narrow ends (diagram 8).

4 Press the completed diamond with the steam iron, turn the diamond over to the calico side of the work and trim strings level with the calico edges (diagram 8). Make all the string diamonds in the same way.

8

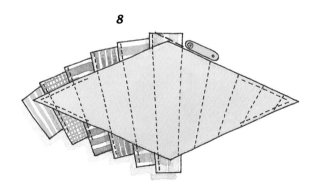

Joining plain strips to string diamonds

1 Stitch the string diamonds to the long plain strips (diagram 9). Make sure that the straight of grain runs in the same direction on all pieces. When stitching has been completed, press the seams towards the plain strips, then cut the sections apart, as shown. This will produce pairs of one plain diamond and one string diamond.

2 Join pairs to make rows (diagram 10). The rows are joined working diagonally across the quilt. Begin each row with a plain diamond and add one at the end of each row (you will need to cut some extra plain diamonds). These edge diamonds will be trimmed to size later.

3 Following the quilt plan, arrange the rows on the floor and number each with a label. Pick up the rows in sequence and machine stitch them together. Press the seams so that they face towards the bottom edge of the quilt. Trim away the excess fabric from the edge diamonds making sure that you leave enough seam allowance on each side.

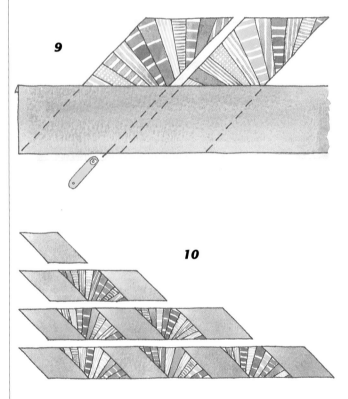

ADDING THE BORDERS

1 For the side borders, measure the quilt from the centre top to centre bottom. Cut two strips of border fabric to this measurement, 9½ in/24.5 cm wide.

2 For the top and bottom borders, measure from centre side edge to centre side edge, before the side borders have been stitched to the quilt. Cut two strips to this measurement, 9½ in/24.5 cm wide.

3 For the corner squares, cut four pieces from the chosen fabric, 9½ in/24.5 cm square. Stitch one square to either end of the top and bottom border strips. Press the seams towards the squares.

4 Stitch first the side, then the top and bottom borders to the quilt top, matching centres. Press seams towards borders.

5 Layer the quilt top, wadding and backing and baste or pin together. Quilt if desired, or tie. I have quilted in-the-ditch round the diamonds and in a zigzag pattern in the border.

6 To finish the quilt make a 2 in/5 cm double bias binding using the continuous strip technique. Press the binding in half lengthwise. Place the raw edges of the binding to the raw edges of the quilt. Using your machine presser foot as a seam guide (width from needle to foot edge), stitch the binding to the front of the quilt. Turn the binding over the raw edge and slip stitch the folded edge of binding to the back of the quilt.

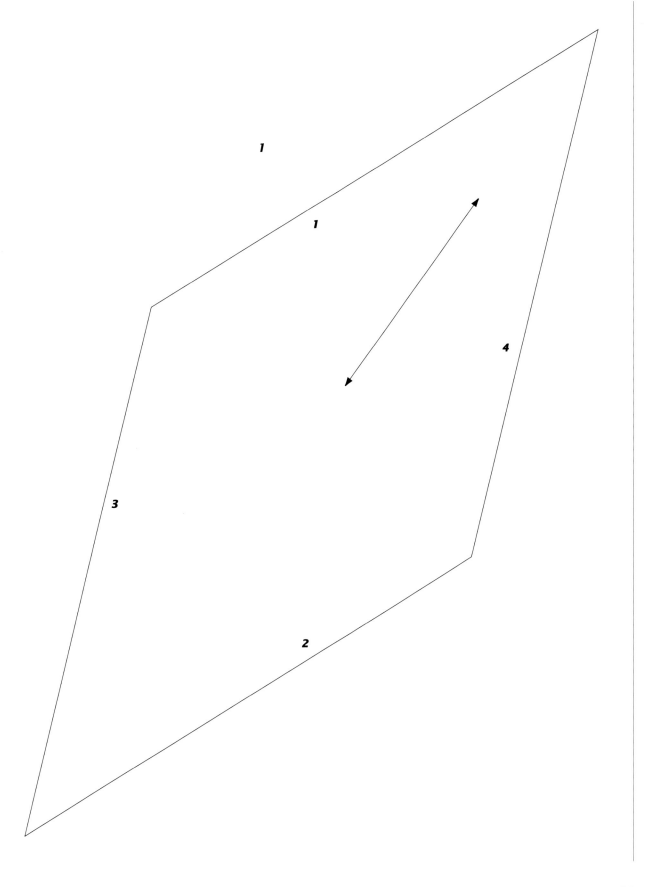

DECORATIVE STITCH SAMPLER

Make this simple "Churn" block patchwork and quilt it with a variety of decorative stitches. It could be used as either a cot quilt or a sampler to hang on the wall. The patchwork is quick to make on the sewing machine and the decorative stitches are easy and therapeutic to work by hand: the whole quilt took about 30 hours. These stitches produce a home-spun, country look rather than a fine quilted effect.

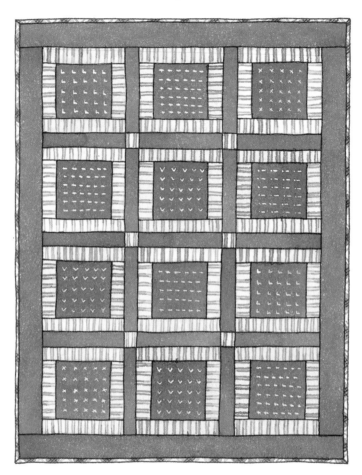

Quilt size: 35 x 45 in/89 x 114.5 cm

MATERIALS

All fabrics used in the quilt top are 45 in/115 cm wide.

Navy fabric: 1 yard/1 metre
Striped fabric: ¾ yard/70 cm
Backing: 40 x 48 in/100 x 120 cm
Wadding: cotton, 40 x 48 in/100 x 120 cm ("Warm and Natural" is recommended)

Quilting thread: "coton à broder" or similar embroidery thread in a contrasting colour for the decorative stitches
Needles: assorted length with an eye large enough to take embroidery thread
Check binding fabric: 24 x 24 in/60 cm x 60cm

CUTTING

1 Using the navy fabric and cutting across the width of the fabric, cut three strips 6½ x 26 in/16.5 x 66 cm (diagram 1).

1

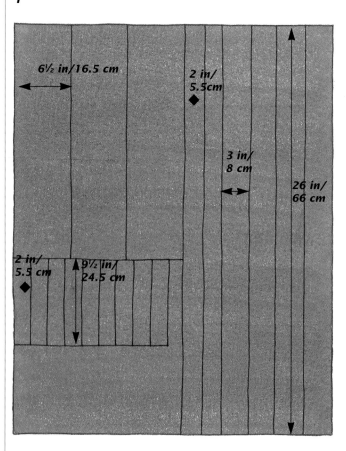

2 Cut nine short strips each 2 x 9½ in/5.5 x 24.5 cm. These are for joining the blocks.

3 From the remaining navy fabric and still cutting across the full width of the fabric, cut two strips, 2 in/5.5 cm wide for joining the rows and four strips, 3 in/8 cm wide for the borders.

4 Using the striped fabric and cutting across the full width of the fabric across the stripes, cut thirteen 2 in/5.5 cm strips. These are for bordering the navy squares and for making the small striped squares which connect the completed blocks.

STITCHING

1 Take six of the 2 in/5.5 cm striped strips and trim them so that they each measure 2 x 26 in/5.5 x 66 cm. Stitch them to each of the long sides of the 6½ in/16.5 cm wide navy strips (diagram 2). Press the seams towards the striped fabric.

2

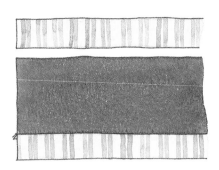

2 Cut these bordered sections again every 6½ in/16.5 cm, to make 12 blocks (diagram 3).

3

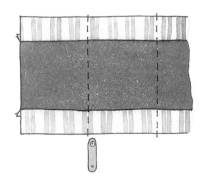

3 From the remaining striped fabric strips, cut 24 short strips 9½ in/24.5 cm. Stitch these borders to the sides of each of the 12 blocks (diagram 4). Press the seams towards the striped fabric.

4

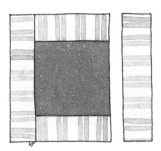

4 Using the scraps left over from the striped strips, cut six connecting squares, each 2 x 2 in/5.5 x 5.5 cm.

5 Take two of the navy 2 x 9½ in/5.5 x 24.5 cm pieces and join the first three blocks together to make the first row. Repeat, until you have completed four rows of three blocks (diagram 5). One strip will be left over which will be used in the following step.

5

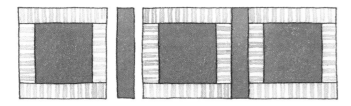

6 From the remaining 2 in/5.5 cm navy long strips, cut eight more short strips each measuring 9½ in/24.5 cm. Join the short strips to the connecting squares, also using the strip left over from step 5 (diagram 6). When the strips are complete, join the four rows of blocks together with these strips in between. Press the seams towards the striped borders.

6

ADDING THE BORDERS

1 Measure the quilt top from centre top to centre bottom. From two of the 3 in/8 cm navy strips, cut two borders to this length. Stitch these borders to each of the long sides of the quilt. Press the seams towards the centre of the work.

2 For the top and bottom borders, measure from centre side edge to centre side edge. Cut borders from the two remaining 3 in/8 cm navy strips to this measurement. Stitch the top and bottom borders to the quilt and press the seams towards the striped borders.

FINISHING THE QUILT

1 Layer the backing, wadding and quilt top, then baste the layers together.

2 Work the decorative stitches, using the embroidery thread and large-eyed needle. Place the work in a quilting hoop and begin by quilting the centre blocks and working out to the edges of the quilt. Following the stitch diagrams, work the different stitches creating two blocks of each stitch.

3 Some of the stitches are worked in rows from top to bottom and others are worked from right to left (opposite direction for left-handed stitchers). To start, knot one end of the thread and pop the knot through the top layer of fabric so that it remains hidden between the layers. To finish, make a knot close to the last stitch and pull the needle and thread between the layers. Bring the needle out a short distance away, then pop the knot through the top fabric and trim the thread. Make sure the end is hidden in the quilt layers. Note that the stage **B** to **C** stitch (see stitch diagrams) will appear on the back of the work.

4 To finish the quilt, make a 2 in/5 cm double bias binding using the continuous strip technique. Press the binding in half lengthwise. Place the raw edges of the binding to the raw edges of the quilt. Using your machine presser foot as a seam guide (width from needle to foot edge), stitch the binding to the front of the quilt. Turn the binding over the raw edge and slip stitch the folded edge of binding to the back of the quilt.

❝On small blocks I work decorative stitches in rows approximately 1 in/2.5 cm apart with stitches about ½ – ¾ in/1–2 cm apart. On a large quilt both rows and stitches can be spaced further apart. I like to place the stitches "by eye" to give the work a more naïve and less organised effect, but do use chalk lines if you prefer to stitch on a guideline.❞

BIG STITCH QUILTING PATTERNS

Cross stitch (diagram 7)

1 Working from top to bottom, bring the needle out at **A**. Stitch from **B** to **C** through all layers.

2 Insert the needle at **D** and passing the needle through top layers only, bring it out again at a new point **A** to begin the next stitch.

Single buttonhole/Blanket stitch (diagram 8)

1 Working from top to bottom, bring the needle out **A** and make a loop with thread. Stitch from **B** to **C** through all layers.

2 Insert the needle at **D** to hold the loop, then push the needle between the layers bringing the needle out at a new point **A** to begin the next stitch.

Methodist knot (diagram 9)

1 Working from right to left (similar to a back-stitch), bring the needle out at **A**. Stitch from **B** to **C** through all layers.

2 Insert the needle at **D** to make a small back stitch, then push the needle between the layers bringing it out at a new point **A** to begin the next stitch.

Mennonite tacks (diagram 10)

1 Working from right to left, bring the needle out at **A**. Stitch from **B** to **C** through all layers.

2 Take the needle back down at **D** to form a small vertical bar across the first stitch and passing the needle through top layers only, bring it out again at a new point **A** to begin the next stitch.

Crow footing or Fly stitch (diagram 11)

1 Working from top to bottom and spacing the stitches about 2 in/5.5 cm apart, bring the needle out at **A**, then loop the thread and stitch from **B** to **C** through all layers.

2 Take the needle back down at **D** to secure the loop of the first stitch. Passing the needle through top layers only, bring it out again at a new point **A** to begin the next stitch.

" Make these stitches about ¼–⅜ in/6 mm–1 cm long. If they are much larger they'll look clumsy. "

Utility quilting (diagram 12)

This is quicker to work than traditional quilting and produces a softer look than machine quilting. It is extremely suitable for country quilts.

1 These small, even running stitches should be of a consistent length, between ⅛ and ¼ in/3 and 6 mm. The thickness of both fabric and thread will affect the length of the stitch. Work in straight rows, as I have done, or in a free-hand zigzag from right to left.

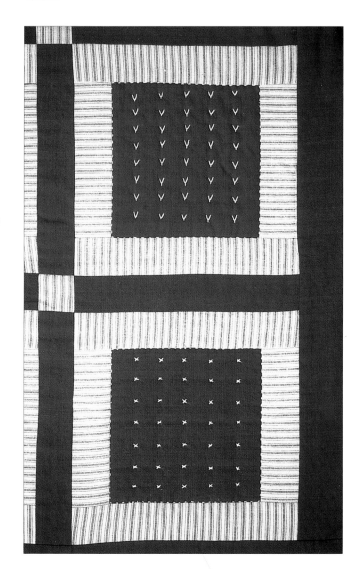

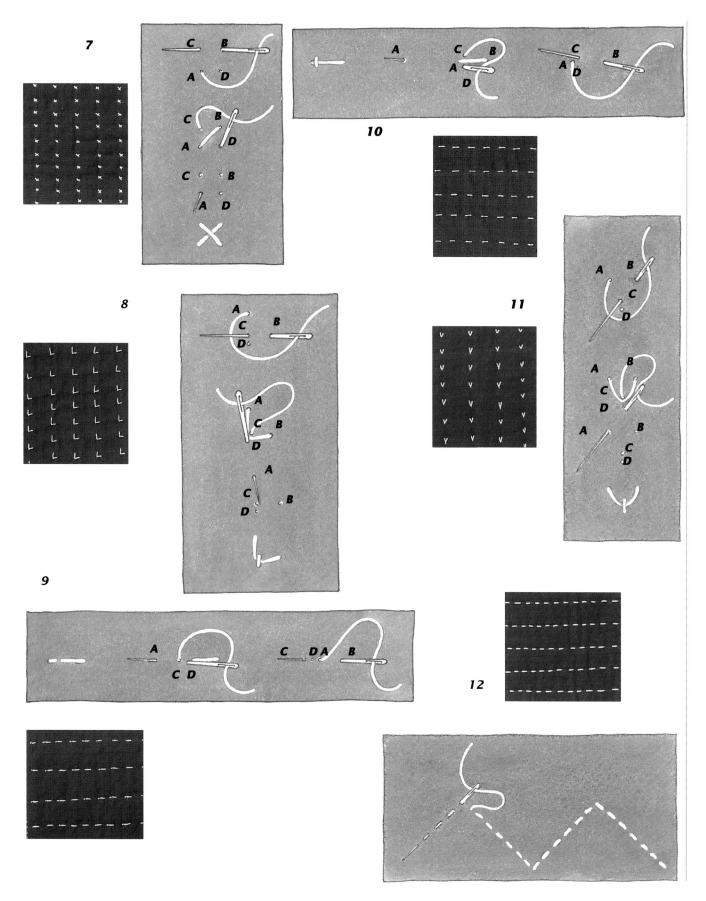

7

8

9

10

11

12

A PIECE OF SUMMER

Sunny summery days are captured in this lively quilt made from 1930s reproduction fabrics: bubble-gum pink, lemon yellow, bright green and tomato red with only the plain calico providing a calming influence. This is a version of "Broken Dishes", a block pattern that was often used in early quilts. If repeated blocks of this design are set in an "edge to edge" arrangement and made from multi-patterned fabrics, then it will produce an overall effect of fragments of china. Here the block is arranged alternately with large squares and this gives a strong diagonal slant to the design. The quilt is very simple and quick to piece. It will take about 30 hours. It will make a bright top quilt for a bed or throw for a sofa.

Quilt size: 68½ x 52½ in/171.5 x 132 cm

MATERIALS

All fabrics used in the quilt top are 45 in/115 cm wide.

Pieced squares: pink, 18 in/50 cm; green (A), 18in/ 50 cm; plain calico, 27 in/70 cm
Large squares: green (B), 9 in/25 cm; yellow, 9 in/ 25 cm; blue (A), 9 in/25 cm; blue (B), 9 in/25 cm

Border: red print, 60 in/150 cm
Ribbon: 1 x 50 g ball cotton knitting ribbon for mock ties
Wadding: cotton, 72 x 56 in/184 x 145 cm ("Warm and Natural" is recommended)
Backing: 72 x 56 in/184 x 145 cm
Binding: beige, 24 in/60 cm square

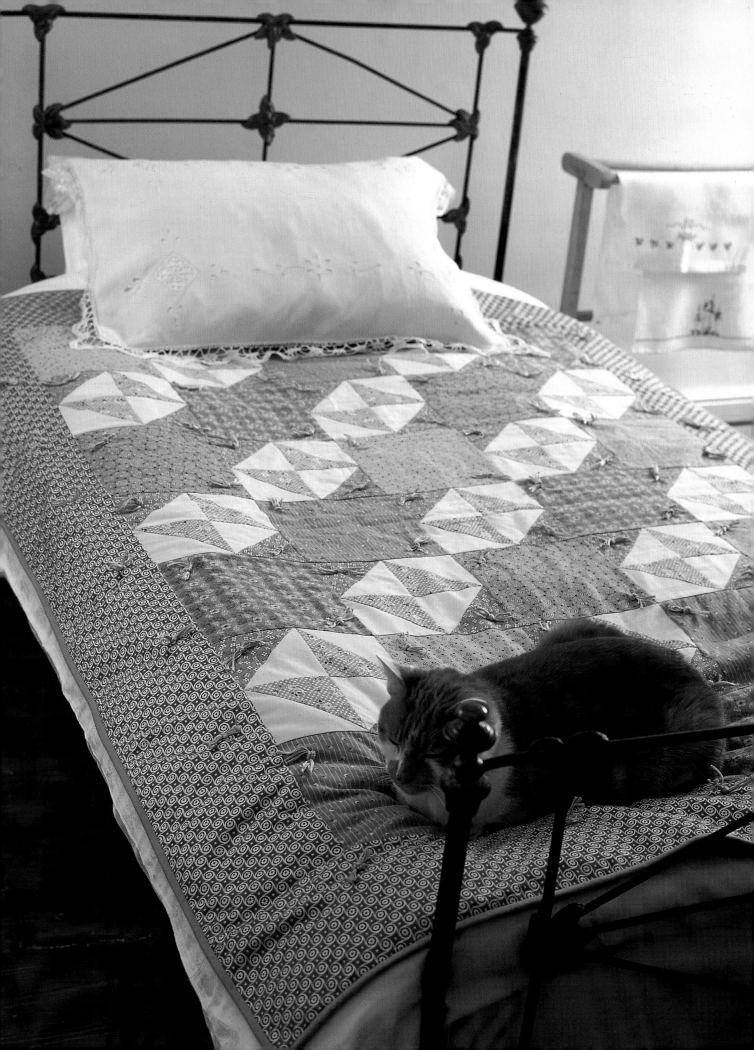

PIECED SQUARES
Cutting
1 Cut 17 pink squares, 17 green (**A**) squares and 34 calico squares, all 5 x 5 in/13 x 13 cm.

Stitching
1 Place the squares right sides together, pairing one square of either pink or green (**A**) to one calico square to make 34 pairs in total.

2 Draw a pencil line diagonally from corner to corner. Machine stitch either side of the diagonal line (diagram 1) using the width from the machine needle to the edge of the presser foot as a seam allowance.

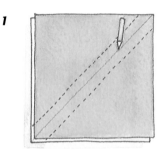

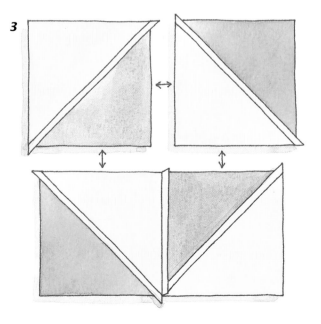

3 Repeat the process with the other squares, using the chain-piecing method. Doing this cuts out the need to break the thread and restart with each new set of squares.

4 When all the squares have been stitched, snip them apart, then cut along the diagonal lines (diagram 2a). You will now have new squares made up of two triangles: one patterned and one calico (diagram 2b). Press all the seams towards the patterned fabric.

5 Trim the pieced squares to the correct size: 4½ in/11.5 cm square.

> For step 2, place a pair of squares (calico piece uppermost) on a piece of fine sandpaper to prevent the fabrics from slipping.

6 Join two pieced squares together. Press the seams towards the patterned fabric, then join the pairs (diagram 3).

7 Complete all 17 pieced blocks in the same way. Press the seams.

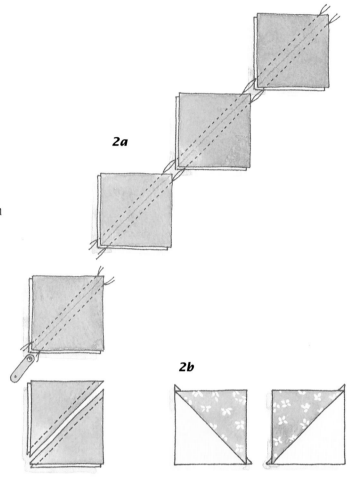

> ❝I like to make these pieced units a little on the large side, then trim them to the required size once the first machining stage has been completed.❞

LARGE SQUARES
Cutting

1 From the remaining pieces of coloured fabric, cut the large squares. These should be cut the same size as the completed pieced blocks, i.e. 8½ in/21.5 cm square. Measure the completed pieced blocks and if necessary adjust the measurement for the large squares.

2 From each of the blue fabrics (**A** and **B**), cut five large squares. From the yellow and green (**B**) fabrics, cut four large squares each.

Stitching

1 Following the quilt plan, join the blocks into rows. Press the seams away from the pieced squares. Stitch the rows together. Press the seams.

ADDING THE BORDERS

1 Determine the length of the two side borders by measuring the quilt top from centre top edge to centre bottom edge. Cut two borders to this measurement, 6½ in/16.5 cm wide, from the red fabric.

2 Stitch the borders to the quilt sides. Press the seams towards the borders.

3 Determine the length for the top and bottom borders by measuring the quilt top from centre side edge to centre side edge. Cut two borders to this measurement, 6½ in/16.5 cm wide, from the red fabric.

4 Stitch the borders to the top and bottom edges of the quilt and press the seams towards the borders.

FINISHING THE QUILT

1 Cut 96 lengths of ribbon for the mock ties, each 16 in/ 40 cm long.

2 This ribbon will be too thick to pull through the quilt layers, so make mock ties as follows: fold the lengths in half and then in half again and tie two knots in the middle, one on top of the other. Snip through the loops at the ends.

3 Layer the quilt top, wadding and backing, and baste or pin the layers together.

4 Stitch each mock tie in place (see quilt plan) by making a firm backstitch through all quilt layers, then stitch the tie securely to the quilt; finish with a couple of back stitches hidden under the knot of the tie. Finish the quilt with a double bias binding using the continuous strip technique.

WINTER WALL

This rustic quilt was created from a variety of tweed and suiting samples arranged in a "brick wall" design. These samples originally came from the workroom of a high class tailor and were passed on to me by a friend. The colours and textures of the tweeds evoke a strong feeling of the countryside in winter: frozen landscapes, leaden skies and trees stripped bare of their leaves. The borders are made from a remnant of silk tweed. This warm lap quilt would give solace on a stormy night. In the past utility quilts and comforters were often made from old clothing, remnants, scraps left over from dressmaking and fabrics saved from swatch cards. The quilts were sometimes lined with old blankets but this one is padded with a thin wadding. It took roughly 20 hours.

◆

Quilt size: 61½ x 54 in/156 x 137 cm

MATERIALS

A bag of scraps or sample fabrics (bag approximately the size of a small pillowcase, see method for sizes)
Small sticky labels: for labelling the rows
Border fabric: wool, ¾ yard/70 cm, 60 in/152 cm wide
Backing: brushed cotton or similar, 64 x 58 in/163 x 148 cm (if possible, use 60 in/150 cm wide fabric for the backing as it will save joining narrower pieces)

Wadding: thin, 64 x 58 in/163 x 153 cm
Quilting thread: extra strong or buttonhole thread
Needles: long needles with an eye large enough to take the thick thread

DESIGNING

Clear a space on the floor and arrange the pieces in rows in a "brick wall" formation, referring to the quilt plan. You will need a total of 85 rectangles and 12 "half" rectangles. Don't cut these to size yet, just tuck under the spare fabric until you are happy with the arrangement. Arrange the pieces making 13 rows. Look again at the illustration and you will see that every other row begins and ends with a "half" rectangle and also that I have arranged light and dark rectangles alternately.

> To view the full effect of your arrangement, look at it through a reducing glass, a front door spy glass or through the wrong end of binoculars; this way you will quickly see if the design works.

CUTTING

1 When you are happy with the arrangement, trim all the samples to the required size. The pieces for this quilt all measured $6\frac{1}{2}$ x $4\frac{1}{2}$ in/16.5 x 11.5 cm.

2 Cut the half rectangles to size but don't be tempted just to cut the rectangles in half, remember that you will need to allow for seam allowances. So if, for example, your large rectangle measures $6\frac{1}{2}$ x $4\frac{1}{2}$ in/16.5 x 11.5 cm, then you will need to make the "half" rectangles $3\frac{1}{2}$ x $4\frac{1}{2}$ in/9 x 11.5 cm.

3 As you pick up the pieces for trimming, take care not disturb your design. When all the pieces have been trimmed, carefully stack the pieces in rows and use the sticky labels to number each row. Hold the pieces for each row together with a clothes peg or large clip.

STITCHING

1 Pick up one row at a time and stitch the rectangles, joining the short edges together, still keeping the pieces in strict order. Press the seams open. (Because these suiting samples are thicker than fabrics normally used for quiltmaking, it would be extremely bulky if the seams were pressed in one direction only.) Leave the label in place but do not iron on top of it as this may leave a sticky mark.

2 Replace the completed row, then pick up, stitch and press the next one in the same way. Continue until all the rectangles have been joined, making 13 rows.

3 Stitch the rows together, again taking care not to disturb the order of the arrangement.

ADDING THE BORDERS

1 To determine the measurements for the side borders, measure the pieced quilt top from centre top to centre bottom including the seam allowances.

2 Using this measurement, cut two strips from the border fabric, each $6\frac{1}{2}$ in/16.5 cm wide, then stitch to the quilt and press the seams open.

3 For the top and bottom borders, measure the quilt from centre side edge to centre side edge, including the seam allowances.

4 Using this measurement, cut two borders each $6\frac{1}{2}$ in/ 16.5 cm wide. Machine stitch to top and bottom ends of the quilt and press the seams open.

FINISHING THE QUILT

1 Position the completed quilt top carefully onto the backing and wadding (with the wadding in the middle). Make sure that you leave a clear 3 in/7.5 cm of wadding and backing fabric showing on all sides beyond the edges of the quilt top. This will be used for finishing the quilt. Pin and baste through all layers.

2 Using a thick thread and large needle, quilt along the horizontal seam lines using either Utility quilting or Mennonite tacks (see page 63).

3 To quilt the border, use masking tape to make guidelines and frame the pieced section of the quilt with four or five rows of Utility Quilting.

4 To finish the quilt, trim away excess wadding and backing, leaving 2in/5 cm showing. Fold the backing and wadding over to the front of the work, placing raw edge of backing to raw edge of quilt top. Fold over again to form a 1 in/2.5 cm final border. Baste, then finish with slip stitch or blanket stitch.

SIMPLE and SERENE

These are the two qualities in nature and the surrounding countryside that I value most and that I have incorporated into my quilts. These are also qualities much favoured by the Japanese and reflected in their textile designs. This mutual interest led me to find out more about the influences on Japanese designs and motifs. The resulting ideas are reflected in these quilts.

Many Japanese live in crowded cities, due to the scarcity of habitable land on their group of islands. As genuine quiet can be so scarce, they have developed beliefs to cultivate inner space and peace. Besides allowing them to enjoy the beauties of nature as if in private while in the midst of a crowd, this also allows them to imagine forested mountainsides when contemplating a moss-covered rock set in a serene garden, only a few feet square. The majority of their motifs are inspired by natural forms. They are also very conscious of the weather and the passing seasons and will turn up en masse at specific sites to view cherry blossom or irises in bloom.

Simple designs; inner serenity: pleasures which I hope you will find while working the following quilts.

— JENNI DOBSON

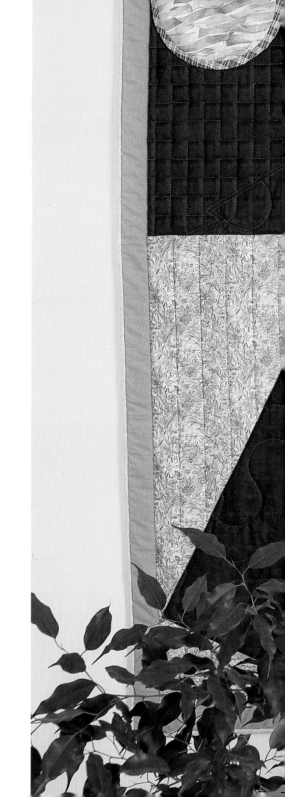

PACIFIC KIMONO

Having read that Japanese nobility slept on the floor under ordinary clothing at a time roughly corresponding to the western Medieval period, I felt compelled to make a quilt that looked like a kimono for our own bed! Making a large version of Sawako Tsurugiji's charming kimono block seemed a perfect and speedy answer. This is the result; with its lightweight filling it's ideal for a bed covering in warm weather.

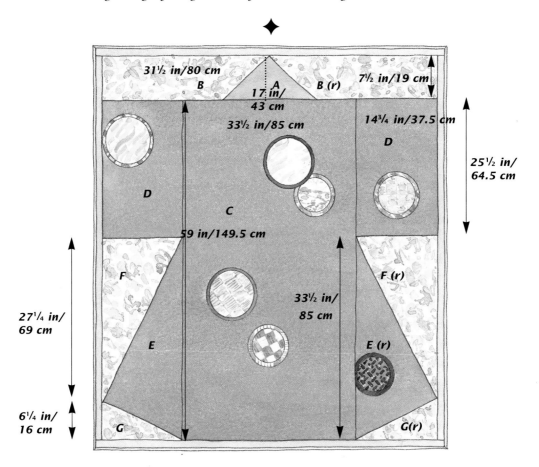

Quilt size: 68 x 71½ in/174 x 182.5 cm

MATERIALS

Dark blue fabric for kimono: (with a woven geometric design to save marking a quilting design) 4 yards/3.8 metres, 45 in/115 cm wide

Background fabric: printed cotton, 1½ yards/ 1.4 metres, 45 in/115 cm wide

Faded crimson for collar: 1 fat quarter

Border fabric: light blue, ⅝ yard/60 cm, 45 in/115 cm wide

Binding fabric: light yellow, ¼ yard/25 cm, 45 in/ 115 cm wide

Scraps of print and plain fabric for rings, fillings and chequerboards: eleven squares for the rings and filling fabrics, none greater than 11 x 11 in/28 x 28 cm; six strips for chequerboards, none greater than 21 x 2½ in/54 x 6.5 cm.

Card or template plastic

Backing: 2¼ yards/2 metres, 80 in/203 cm wide

Lightweight wadding: 1 double bed size piece

Masking tape: 2 in wide

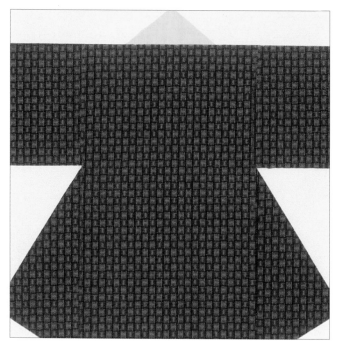

ALTERNATIVE COLOUR SCHEMES

Changing the three basic colours of the kimono block alters the balance and appearance of the design in interesting ways. Red is a felicitous colour in Japan, often featuring on traditional wedding kimono, for example. Set it against a neutral grey background, with sparkling black and white fabrics for the appliqué blocks. Alternatively, choose a multi-coloured plaid for the kimono, selecting one of the darker colours for the background, then find solids in the rest of the colours for the accent rings. A neutral background combined with a low-key chestnut print would make a very liveable-with quilt. Tans, rusts and an accent of yellow lifts this colour scheme out of the commonplace. Fresh with the coolness of the ocean, the turquoise colour scheme benefits from the accent of geranium.

The kimono is decorated with a few simply appliquéed rings, containing strip-pieced chequerboards or just showcasing attractive pieces of fabric. Of course, the idea of working a whole quilt as a large version of one block isn't totally new – think of the Amish favourite, "Diamond in a Square" – but I think it's one that suits the quilter in a hurry, as the top for this quilt was assembled and decorated in two days. I made the body of the kimono using a subtle satin-woven check fabric which eliminated the need to mark the "juji-tsunagi" sashiko design quilted across the top part of the kimono. I chose to hand-quilt (not in a week-end!) but this design eminently suits machine-quilting. I chose to stitch a related curved pattern, known as "chidori-tsunagi", in the lower half, but a quicker alternative would be to follow the woven lines of the fabric to machine-quilt the first pattern over the whole of the kimono.

For the curious, the quilt owes its name to a visit I made to the Pacific coast of California around the towns of Carmel and Monterey. The deep blue fabric for the kimono, originally chosen for its suitability as a quilting grid, reminded me of the ocean there and I decided to colour-scheme the whole quilt around my memories of a beautiful day – sun-bleached rocks, faded paint on wooden buildings, etc. The seven rings scattered over this quilt are my choice – work your own to suit the fabrics you have chosen. As I quilted it, I realised that the pine trees at the top of the beach in Carmel were missing. Though it was too late to add their dark green to the colour palette, because pines are such a favourite motif in Japan, I was able to quilt little stylized branches of them between the shoulders on the back of my kimono as the important back protector!

CUTTING

1 Following the measurements on the quilt plan, draw up the rectangular areas **A** - **B** and **E** - **F** - **G** on large pieces of paper and cut them apart to make patterns for shapes **A** to **F**.

2 From the dark blue kimono fabric, cut one **C** rectangle (kimono back), 34 x 59½ in/87 x 152 cm and two **D** rectangles (sleeves), 26 x 15¼ in/67 x 39 cm.

3 Using pattern piece **E** and adding ¼ in/0.75 cm seam allowance on all sides, cut one triangle **E** and one of **E** reversed (kimono fronts), also from the dark blue.

4 From the background fabric and using the prepared patterns with ¼ in/0.75 cm seam allowance added to all sides of all pieces, cut one each of pieces **B**, **F** and **G** and one of each in reverse: **B(r)**, **F(r)** and **G(r)**.

5 Fold the faded crimson in half and place pattern piece **A** with the centre line to the fold, then add ¼ in/0.75 cm seam allowance on outer edges and cut one collar **A**.

6 From the full width of the light blue border fabric, cut strips 2½ in/7 cm wide to be used at a later stage to make up four borders, 70 in/178 cm long.

7 For the binding, from the full width of the yellow fabric, cut strips 1 in/2.5 cm wide to a total 8 yards/7.5 metres.

8 For two 10 in/25.5 cm rings, cut four squares 11 x 11 in/ 28 x 28 cm, two of ring fabric and two of filling fabric.

9 For two 9 in/ 23 cm chequerboard rings, cut two squares 10 x 10 in/25.5 x 25.5 cm of ring fabric and two pairs of strips, each strip 21 x 2½ in/54.5 x 6.5 cm.

10 For two 8 in/20 cm rings, cut four squares 9 x 9 in/23 x 23 cm, two of ring fabric and two of filling fabric.

11 For one 7 in/18 cm chequerboard ring, cut one square 8 x 8 in/20 x 20 cm and two strips each 13 x 1½ in/35 x 4 cm.

STITCHING
Plain filled rings

1 Either using the ring patterns provided (diagram 1 on page 77) or drawing your own with a pair of compasses, make templates from card or plastic for the sizes of ring required. I have used four sizes of ring with a diameter of 7, 8, 9 and 10 in/ 18, 20, 23 and 25.5 cm. Include the vertical and horizontal register marks.

2 Iron the squares of ring and filling fabric, then finger-press vertical and horizontal folds in both (diagram 2).

2

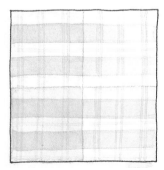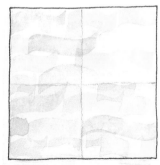

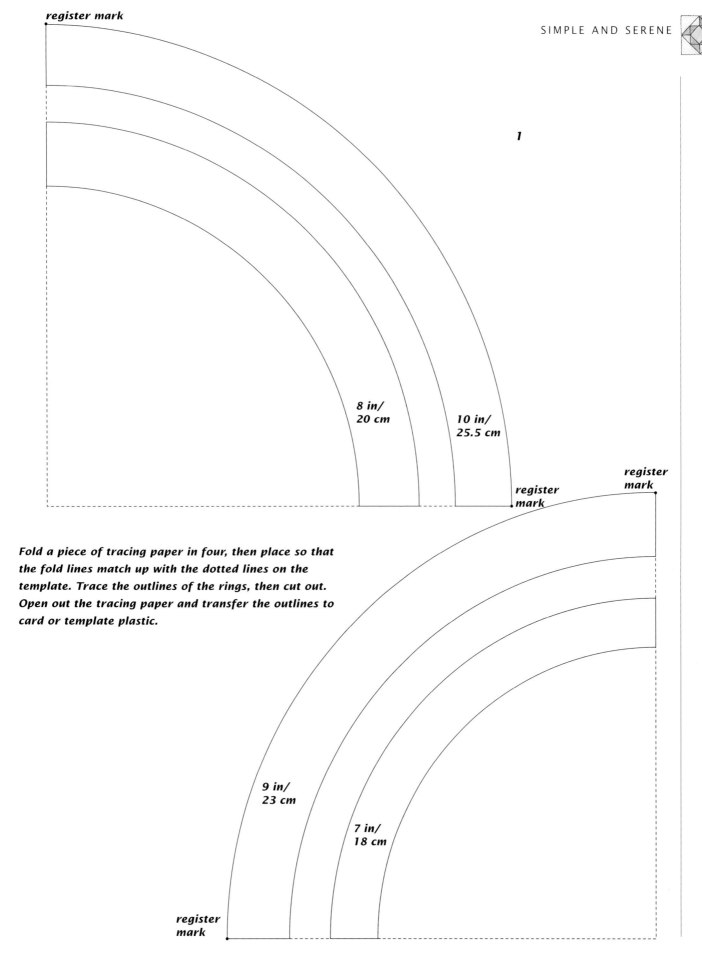

register mark

1

8 in/
20 cm

10 in/
25.5 cm

register
mark

register
mark

Fold a piece of tracing paper in four, then place so that
the fold lines match up with the dotted lines on the
template. Trace the outlines of the rings, then cut out.
Open out the tracing paper and transfer the outlines to
card or template plastic.

9 in/
23 cm

7 in/
18 cm

register
mark

3 Line up the register marks on the ring template with these creases on the right side of the ring fabric; draw in the concentric circles of the ring (diagram 3).

3

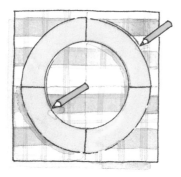

4 Place the marked ring fabric, right side up, over the right side of the filling fabric. Pin, then baste carefully between the two concentric circles (diagram 4).

4

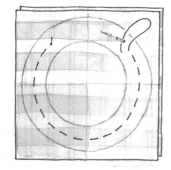

5 Cut away the fabric from inside the ring, leaving a scant ¼ in/0.75 cm turning (diagram 5). Clip the seam allowance just near the vertical and horizontal register marks where the grain is straightest (diagram 6). If you clip all round the curve, this may become too stretched and will be more difficult to stitch down neatly. Fold under the turning and blind-hem.

5

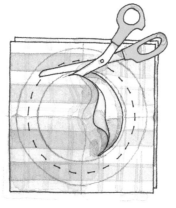

6

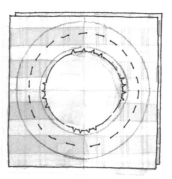

6 After stitching the inside of the ring, use the basting stitches as a guide to trim away the excess filling fabric from just outside the basting stitches. It may help to crease lightly along the outer drawn line as a guide also.

7 Place the ring on the kimono panel of the quilt, pin and baste in place. Trim the excess fabric from around the outer ring and blind-hem to the panel. Instead of stitching on the rings as you prepare them, you might like to prepare several up to step 6, then spread out the kimono panels and play around with the arrangement of the rings to find an arrangement that pleases you. Japanese design favours having some partly hidden, either by overlapping them (as in the back panel of the kimono featured) or, rather than centring them, having some slipping into a seam (as with the ring on the right front.)

Chequerboard filled rings
The wider strips make a chequerboard to fit the 9 in/23 cm rings and the narrower strips make a chequerboard to fit the 7 in/18 cm ring.

1 Place a pair of strips, right sides together, and stitch with a ¼ in/0.75cm seam. Press seam towards the darker fabric.

2 Cross-cut the assembled strip into slices of the same width as the original strips (diagram 7a).

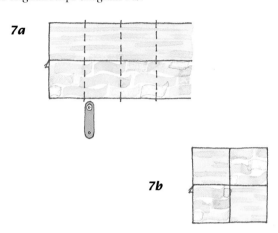

7a

7b

3 Stitch the slices together in pairs, reversing the colours (diagram 7b). Stitch two pairs together to make two rectangles of four-by-two squares. Press, then join these units to make a four-by-four chequerboard (diagram 7c).

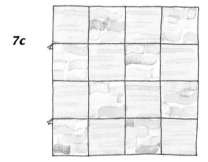

7c

4 Use the centre seam lines for registering the ring fabric over the chequerboard, then baste, trim and blind-hem the ring as before.

ASSEMBLING THE QUILT TOP
1 After stitching the rings to the panels, use the quilt plan to lay out all the pieces for the enlarged block.

2 With ¼ in/0.75 cm seam allowances, stitch the panels together as follows:
B to **A** to **Br** for unit **1**; **F** to **E**, then **G** to **E** for unit **2**; **Fr** to **Er**, then to **Gr** for unit **2r**. Press the seams.

3 Stitch one panel **D** (sleeve) to the top of unit **2** and another to unit **2r**. Press.

4 Stitch one of these to each long side of panel **C** (kimono back). Press before adding unit **1** across the top.

ADDING THE BORDERS
1 If necessary join strips to make the borders, then attach them to the completed block.

FINISHING THE QUILT
I divided the kimono featured into upper and lower parts using a zigzag line marked with ¼ in masking tape. Above this I stitched the stepped and crossed pattern "juji-tsunagi" following the woven grid of the fabric (diagram 8). The lower half I stitched with another grid design called "chidori-tsunagi", but as a quicker alternative, I recommend that you quilt the "juji-tsunagi" design all over the kimono.

8

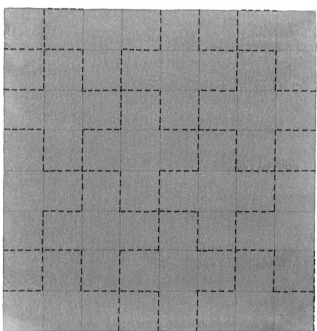

1 Assemble the three layers of backing, wadding and top, then baste or pin.

2 Machine-quilt the chosen designs on the kimono. Quilt the rings in-the-ditch and the background with parallel lines marked using 2 in wide masking tape.

3 After quilting, insert a line of permanent basting in a matching thread to hold the edges of the quilt together before attaching the binding. Sign or label to finish.

SASHIKO INSPIRATIONS 1

Inspired by sashiko stitching, originally used on working jackets for people like firefighters, fishermen and country farmers, this cot quilt in traditional navy and white pays tribute to the technique with a mixture of hand and machine work in a quilt-as-you-stitch method. The quilt took roughly five hours apart from the quilting. I stitched mine by hand with sashiko-style stitching but it would obviously be quicker by machine. Unlike traditional western quilting where the aim is to have the stitch and space next to it equal in size, in sashiko the space is as small as is practical on the fabric being used and the stitch about twice as big. This makes the technique ideal for a speedy project and it is even quicker here because the main focus of this cot quilt is a boldy enlarged sashiko pattern interpreted in machine-couched cotton knitting yarn.

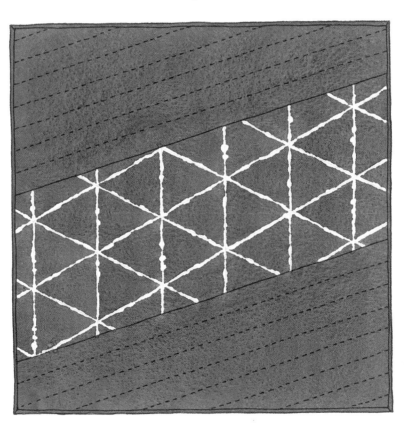

Quilt size: 34 x 34 in/86 x 86 cm

MATERIALS

Plain navy cotton fabric: 1 yard/1 metre, 45 in/ 115 cm wide
Toning backing: 1 yard/1 metre, 45 in/115 cm wide
Wadding: 1¼ yards/115 cm, 45 in/115 cm wide

Clear nylon machine-quilting thread
White, textured cotton knitting yarn: 1 skein
White sashiko thread or coton perlé
Masking tape: 2 in wide

CUTTING

1 Wash and iron the navy fabric and the backing. Trim the selvages from the navy fabric, then cut five 1 in/2.5 cm wide strips from the length of the navy, parallel to the selvage. Put aside for the binding.

2 On the remaining almost square piece of navy, mark two points one 15 in/38 cm down from the top edge on the left-hand side and the other 6 in/15 cm down from the top edge on the right-hand side. With a yard (metre) stick and a suitable marker, connect the two points. Rule a second line parallel to the first about 14 in/35.5 cm away. Cutting along these drawn lines, divide the fabric into unequal thirds and label (diagram 1).

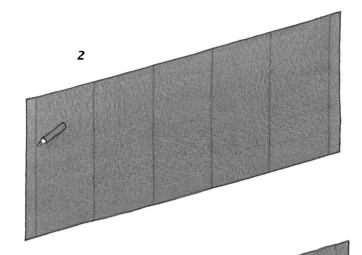

2

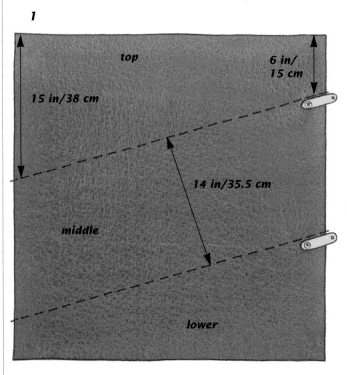

1

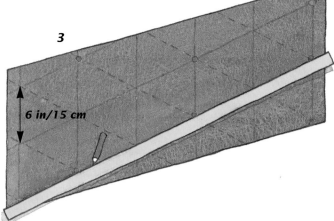

3

> A sharpened sliver of dried soap is good for marking the cutting lines.

MARKING THE QUILT TOP

1 Again with the stick and marker, rule the sashiko grid on the right side of the middle third. Rule the first left-hand vertical about 1¼ in/3.25 cm from the left-hand edge. Rule 6 in/15 cm lines parallel to the selvage (diagram 2).

2 On the second vertical line, mark three points each 6 in/15 cm apart. Using a quilter's rule or set square to keep marks level, repeat on every second vertical in a horizontal line with the first set.

3 With a yard (metre) stick, draw diagonal lines connecting the marks in both directions (diagram 3). Add further parallel lines to cover the whole area.

FINISHING THE QUILT

1 Spread out the backing fabric, right side down, on a flat surface with the wadding on top and centre the marked middle third of the navy, right side up, on top. Check that the top and bottom sections will fit within the area of the backing before safety-pinning the three layers together.

MACHINE-COUCHING

1 Load the sewing machine with a toning thread for the backing in the bobbin and the clear nylon thread on the top. Select the blind-hem stitch on the machine, if available. If not, select a moderately open zigzag but be aware that this will flatten the texture of the yarn more noticeably. Set the width of swing on the zigzag stitch so that it pierces the yarn rather than merely bridging it, which would allow the yarn to be pulled out (diagram 4).

4

5

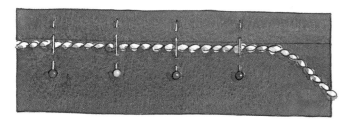

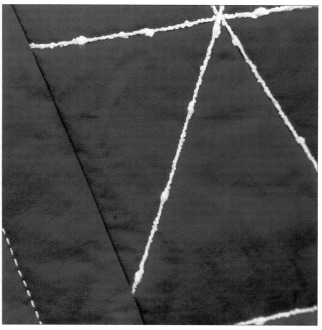

2 Taking care not to stretch the cotton knitting yarn, place the end about 1 in/2.5 cm beyond the first vertical drawn line and place pins at right angles across the yarn to hold it in place down the line (diagram 5). Leave about 1 in/2.5 cm extra at the finish, then cut off. Repeat on all the vertical lines.

3 Couch the yarn in place, stitching all the lines in the same direction. Setting the stitch length to 0 for a few stitches at the start and end of each line of stitching allows you to trim the thread ends without laboriously tying them off or stitching them into the layers.

4 Repeat the process of pinning the yarn in place, then stitching it, first on one diagonal across the panel, then on the other. Remove the safety pins.

5 With right sides together, place the top third of the navy over the top edge of the middle panel, so that when stitched with a ¼ in/0.75 cm seam allowance, the vertical edges will be level. Pin, then stitch. Flip the top section into place over the seam and either finger-press or very lightly press the seam with just the point of the iron, being careful not the crush the wadding. Reposition the safety pins to hold all three layers together in the top third. Repeat with the lower third.

6 Using the sashiko thread or coton perlé, quilt the top and lower thirds with lines of sashiko-style stitching, parallel to the diagonal seams. In the quilt shown, these lines were about 2 in/5 cm apart, marked with wide masking tape. If you prefer a quicker alternative, substitute machine-couched knitting yarn, as in the centre section.

7 After quilting, use navy thread to put in a line of permanent basting stitches close to the edge (i.e. within the ¼ in/0.75 cm seam allowance) all round the quilt. Trim away excess backing and wadding.

8 Join the binding strips, use to bind the quilt, then label to finish.

> ❝ It's a good idea to work a small sample of machine-couching, prepared as directed, to test the best stitch length, width and tension for the chosen fabrics and cotton knitting yarn. The couching stitches should be unnoticeable, and the straight stitches right beside the yarn being couched. ❞

SPRING WALL-HANGING

The Japanese are intensely aware of nature. Certain plants are associated with different months or seasons and symbolize particular characteristics or virtues. Here we have three spring flowers: the violet, the cherry and the iris. The diamond-shaped blocks upon which they are arranged are another popular form, also varied as a stylized cloud. The blocks took me roughly six hours to complete, then four hours for the quilting. The cutting and preparation technique took another afternoon.

Quilt size: 43 x 55 in/109 x 139.5 cm

MATERIALS

Light grey fabric: 1¼ yards/1.2 metres, 45 in/115 cm wide

Inner border fabric: two plain greens, ⅛ yard/10 cm each, 45 in/115 cm wide

Outer border fabric: printed furnishing cotton, ¾ yard/70 cm, 48 in/120 cm wide

Thin paper for tracing the blocks or photocopies

Paper-mounted fusible webbing: 1½ yards/1.4 metres

Flowers, centres and leaves: mixed print and plain scraps

Block background fabrics: seven scrap pieces, none larger than 10 x 7 in/26 x 18 cm

Baking parchment paper

Lightweight interfacing: 1 yard/1 metre

Binding fabric: bright yellow, ¼ yard/30 cm, 45 in/115 cm wide

Wadding: 1¾ yards/1.75 metres, 60 in/150 cm wide

Backing: 1¾ yards/1.75 metres, 60 in/150 cm wide

Masking tape: ⅝ in and ¼ in

Machine embroidery threads

The blocks have been worked using fusible webbing and mounted onto a support of lightweight interfacing. They are most efficiently worked as a set, all the cutting and bonding being done first, before working the satin stitch. Only scraps of fabric are needed for the motifs. Limiting the number of threads for the embroidery will unify a diversity of scraps. The blocks are scattered over a simple, framed background, which is machine-quilted in parallel lines, the narrow ones with added bar-tacks to represent bamboo, another Japanese favourite plant, symbolizing endurance and constancy.

CUTTING

1 From the light grey fabric, cut a rectangle 31 x 42¾ in/ 79 x 108.5 cm.

2 Cut two strips from both plain green fabrics for the inner border, each 1 in/2.5 cm wide, across the width of the cloth.

3 From the printed outer border fabric, cut four strips 6 in/ 15 cm wide, across the width.

4 Enlarge the block designs (diagram 1 on pages 88 and 89) to measure 9 in/23 cm across the widest point on the diamond. Turn each design over, label this the working side and ink over all design lines to give the reverse pattern required. Note that the second cherry design is used twice, once in reverse.

5 Place the fusible webbing, paper side up, over the working side of the designs and trace off all parts of the design separately including the background diamond shape (diagram 2). Leaves and petals butt up together, but the background shape should be a complete outline so that it goes behind the flowers and leaves.

2

6 Cut out each of the separate leaves and flowers from the fusible webbing tracings carefully, then cut out a separate piece for the diamond background shape. Place each in turn on the wrong side of the chosen fabric and bond.

7 Cut out again (diagram 3) and save all the pieces for the block together in an envelope. Repeat to prepare all seven of the appliqué blocks.

3

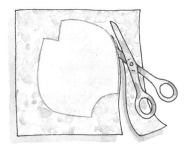

8 From the interfacing, cut one rectangle 11 x 6½ in/ 28 x 17 cm for the iris block, and six rectangles each 10 x 7 in/25 x 18 cm for the other blocks.

9 From the bright yellow binding fabric, cut five strips, 1½ in/4 cm wide, across the fabric and join.

STITCHING

1 Working a block at a time, remove the backing paper from the fused diamond background fabric and bond it to a rectangle of interfacing, following the manufacturer's instructions. Allow to go cold before handling. Remove the backing papers from the rest of the shapes for this block, position them correctly, using the original paper pattern as a guide, then bond. Work all blocks to this stage (diagram 4).

4

2 Set the sewing machine to work a satin-stitch, making a sample first to check the tension. Work all the satin-stitch. Try to plan so that a second colour will cover the ends of the first, and so on. Load one colour at a time and, where possible, work all of one colour where it appears on different blocks. It isn't necessary to have exactly matching threads for each fabric, as repeating a colour helps unify the designs. Cut out each completed block from the interfacing rectangle.

ADDING THE BORDERS

1 Stitch the two lighter green inner border strips to the left-hand side and the top of the light grey rectangle.

2 Stitch the two darker green strips to the right-hand side and the bottom.

3 Attach the outer border strips to the sides of the quilt, trimming the ends level as necessary. Add the outer borders to the top and bottom.

FINISHING THE QUILT

1 Turn over a prepared diamond block, place fusible webbing, paper side up, on top and trace off the block outline, being sure to go right to the edges of the block behind the outer stitching (diagram 5). Cut out and fuse to the back of the block. Repeat for all blocks.

5

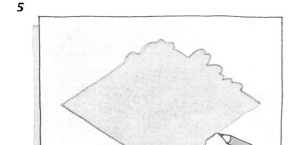

2 Preferably hang the prepared quilt background and arrange the blocks over it. You don't have to copy my design, but note the asymmetry and use of a diagonal flow, both features of Japanese design. Also consider the space around and between the blocks as this is more important to the Japanese eye than the blocks themselves. When you have an arrangement you like, peel off the backing paper and bond each block to the background. Allow each to go cold before moving the background to attach the next.

3 Assemble the quilt top, wadding and backing ready for quilting.

4 Using ⅝ in wide masking tape, mark the bold quilting lines at interesting angles and intervals. Avoid getting them all leaning at the same degree or too equally spaced – the effect you are representing is a stand of bamboo stalks. Also leave space for the narrower stalks.

5 Using a walking or even-feed foot if available and machine embroidery thread, quilt both sides of the masking tape, taking care not to stitch through it and always working from the top of the quilt down. Don't be tempted to turn it and work some from the other direction as this may cause ripples.

6 Remove the masking tape promptly and mark some narrower stalks with ¼ in wide masking tape. Quilt both sides of these, then remove the tape. At intervals on the narrow stalks stitch a bar tack, but without tightening the thread, to represent the joints in the bamboo.

7 Trim the backing and wadding level with the outer border of the quilt top and check that the corners are true. Stitch the bright yellow binding strips to the quilt ⅜ in/1 cm from the edge. Fold over to the back of the work turning in the raw edge and blind-hem to a finished ⅜ in/1 cm.

8 Make and attach a hanging sleeve, then sign or label your quilt to finish.

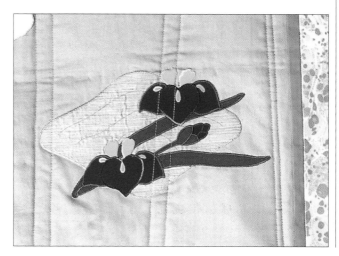

1 *Dotted lines indicate the complete background outline;*
broken lines indicate surface stitching

violet 1

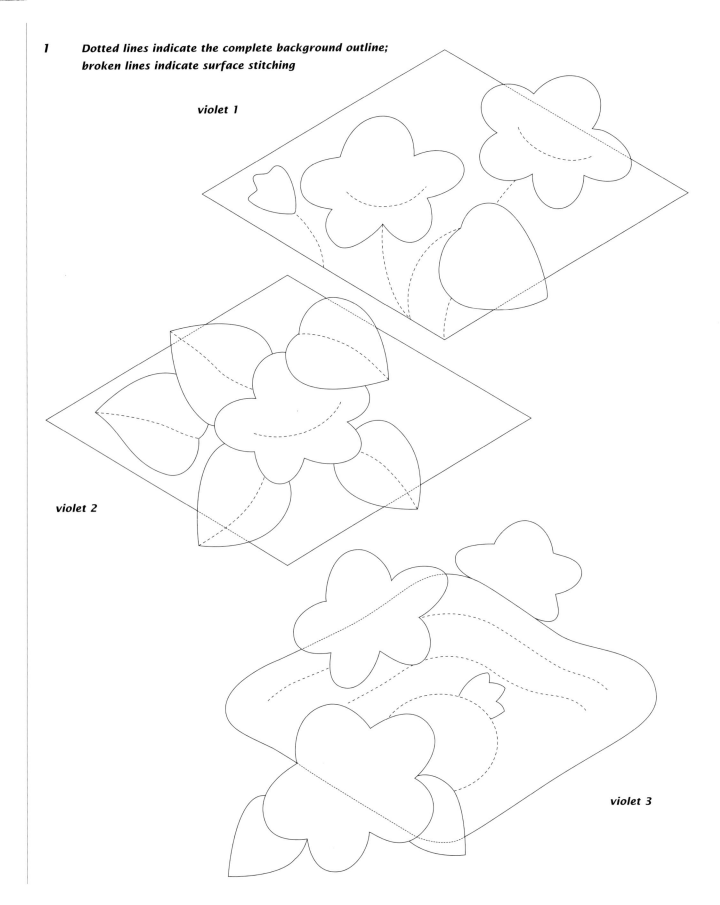

violet 2

violet 3

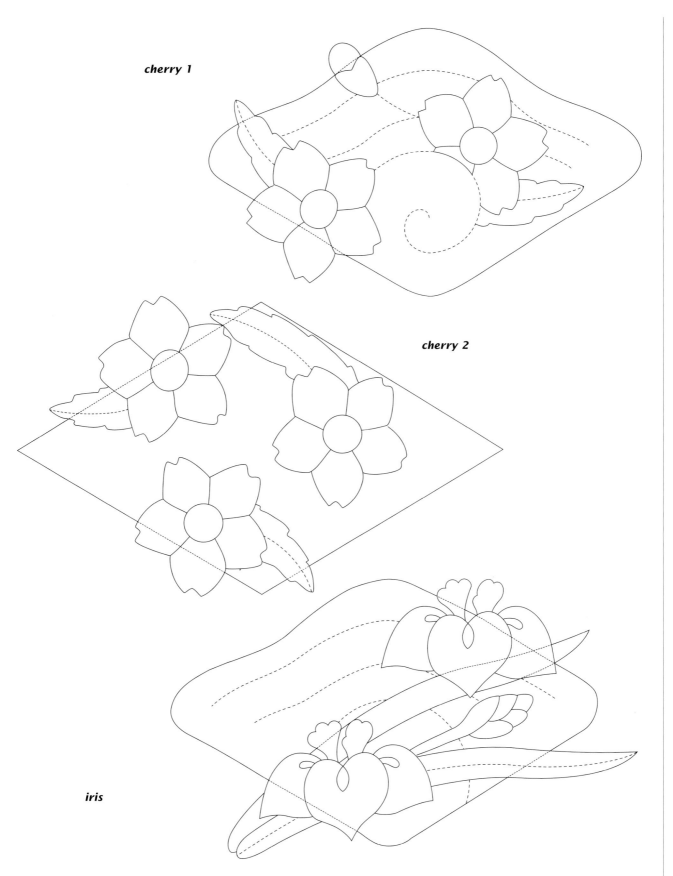

cherry 1

cherry 2

iris

SASHIKO INSPIRATIONS 2

This cot quilt, inspired by a very similar sashiko pattern to that used for Sashiko Inspirations I, acknowledges other Japanese influences too. Firstly, the homespun-looking plaid reflects Japanese textile traditions. Its geometric design also eases the task of marking the quilting pattern. Secondly, the light wadding used in the main part of the quilt (the current preference for baby covers is that they shouldn't be too warm) is balanced by a wide, padded border imitating the padded hems seen on some ceremonial kimono. The sashiko grid, "kagome", is quickly stitched using the longest possible stitch on the machine. Worked in a toning thread, it's so low-key that the stars – formed by whipping some of the gridlines with contrasting embroidery thread – appear as if by magic! The quilt took me approximately seven hours to complete.

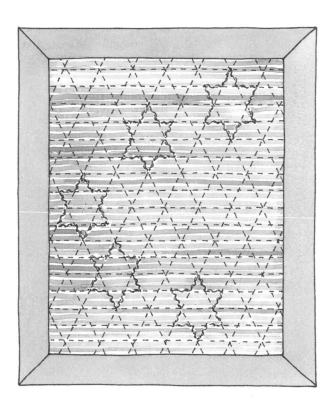

Quilt size: 36 x 42 in/91.5 x 106.5 cm

MATERIALS

All fabrics used in the quilt are 45 in/115 cm wide.

Cotton plaid fabric: 1 yard/1 metre (This could be a stripe if plaids are difficult to find.)
Lightweight wadding: 1¾ yards/1.6 metres

Backing: 1 yard/1 metre
Plain putty fabric: 1 yard/1 metre
Masking tape
Contrast embroidery thread

CUTTING

1 From the plaid fabric, cut a rectangle 30½ x 36 in/ 77.5 x 91.5 cm and matching pieces of wadding and backing.

2 From plain putty fabric, cut two border strips, 7½ x 44 in/ 19 x 112 cm and two strips, 7½ x 38 in/19 x 96.5 cm. Cut matching pieces of wadding.

STITCHING

1 Press the backing, then place, right side down, on a flat surface. Centre over it the wadding and the ironed plaid, right side up. Pin, then baste the layers together.

2 On one long side of the plaid, mark the centre using a line in the weave as a guide. Identify other lines of the pattern at roughly 4 in/10 cm intervals working away from the centre in both directions (diagram 1). Set your machine for the longest possible stitch, then machine-quilt down each of these lines in matching thread.

1

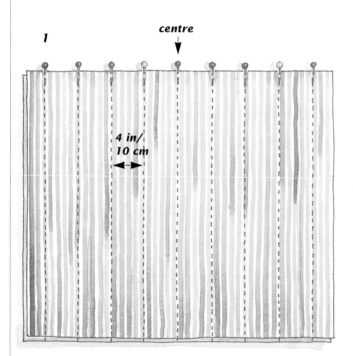

3 Now find the middle of the quilt on one short side. Mark this point with a pin inserted on alternate lines of quilting. At roughly 4 in/10 cm intervals, up and down on the same gridlines, mark more intersections. Place strips of masking tape to connect the pin-marked points diagonally, then machine-quilt these lines (diagram 2). Remove the tape and reposition to connect the same points on the other diagonal. Machine-quilt.

2

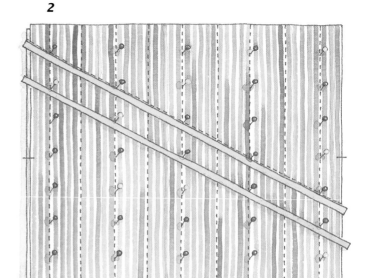

4 Now quilt a final set of lines, parallel to the very first set and halfway between them (diagram 3).

3

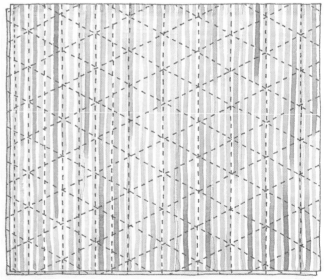

ADDING THE BORDERS

1 Mark a line parallel to and 3 in/7.5 cm in from one long edge on each border strip. Place the wadding strips to the wrong side of the border strips and pin or baste. With the machine still set on a long stitch, machine-baste the marked lines in matching thread. This stitching is to prevent the wadding moving during use and will remain in the border. Machine-baste again on normal stitch length close to both edges.

2 Find the mid-point of each side of the quilt and its respective border. Pin two opposite borders to opposite sides of the centre with right sides facing, taking a $\frac{1}{4}$ in/0.75 cm seam allowance and starting and stopping stitching $\frac{1}{4}$ in/0.75 cm from the corners (diagram 4). Make sure that the machine-basting line across the border will be folded over to the back of the quilt. Folding these borders out of the way where possible, attach the remaining two borders in the same way. Again start and stop stitching 1/4 in/0.75 cm from the corners.

2 Fold the borders over to the back of the quilt, turning in $\frac{1}{4}$ in/0.75 cm to enclose the raw edges. Fold and stitch mitres at the corners on the back as you go.

3 With contrast coloured embroidery thread, whip some of the grid lines to pick out some star shapes (diagram 5). Push the eye of the needle through first to avoid catching any fabric. To keep to Japanese design ideals, work an odd number of stars in an asymmetrical arrangement.

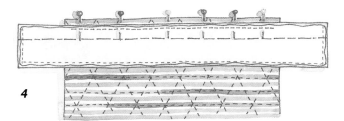

4

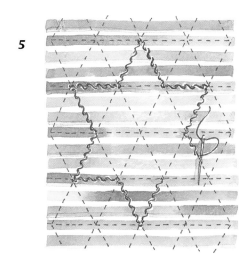

5

FINISHING THE QUILT

1 Fold the excess fabric at the corners of the borders into mitres and stitch. Check that each lies neatly before trimming the excess wadding and fabric.

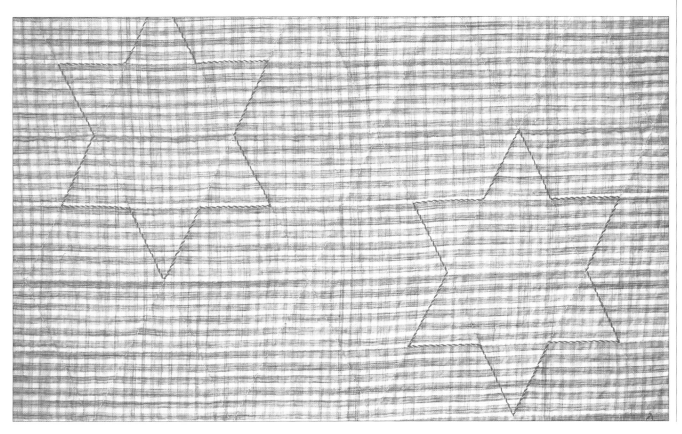

GATEWAYS TO THE PAST

The overall design of this hanging is inspired by the Japanese "screen of state": long hanging panels used to create an illusion of privacy by dividing large rooms yet still allowing people to come and go easily. You can easily adapt the width or length to suit a given space, adding more panels as well as varying their width.

Though this example was made from a gift collection of vintage kimono fabrics, they aren't essential to make this hanging. However, the ancient religion of Shinto holds that everything has a spirit and consequently the Japanese feel that re-using old fabrics means their spirit is being preserved. In the past people made gifts of good fragments from worn kimono to shrines, sometimes to be made into patched robes for monks and sometimes into altar hangings. This prompted the use of a stylized "torii", or shrine gateway, as a feature block.

Quilt size: 47½ x 36 in/120.5 x 91.5 cm

MATERIALS

Backing: printed furnishing cotton fabric, 1⅛ yards/ 1 metre, 48 in/122 cm wide

Thin paper for tracing the block foundations or photocopies

Wadding: needle-punched or compressed, 1⅛ yards/ 1 metre, 60 in/150 cm wide

Binding and hanging sleeves: deep red fabric, 1 yard/ 1 metre, 45 in/115 cm wide

Torii shapes, backgrounds and strips: about 1¾ yards/1.7 metres assorted scraps for piecing, of which five pieces must be about 11 x 9 in/28 x 23 cm

Bamboo pole for hanging: to combined length of panels plus 6 in/15 cm

I took roughly ten hours to do the preparing, block construction and finishing of the panels and a day to do the strip piecing. Your timing will depend on how long you take to assemble and organise the strips.

I decided to theme the panels around different seasons, weather and times of the day. The first panel represents winter and snow. The second shows spring – the dawning of a new year – and the dawn of a new day. The centre panel represents the height of summer and of the day. Panel four is for autumn with its foggy evenings. The last panel shows us dark rainy nights, also of winter. When assembling your own fabrics, try to choose colours and designs associated with the appropriate season but remember not to agonise over every strip! It is only symbolic.

The backing for these panels is cut from a single piece of furnishing fabric, making them reversible should you wish to use them as a divider. The "torii" are worked over paper foundations, which are both easy and quick to work. The rest of each panel is filled with simple strip piecing, a great way to display lots of scraps of wonderful fabrics.

> ❝ If you have never used this method before, make a practice block first from scrap fabrics. Use a short stitch length on the machine, about 15 stitches per inch or 1.75 mm, so that the paper is easy to remove. ❞

CUTTING

1 Divide the furnishing fabric into five panels, each 9½ in/ 24 cm wide and number them, so that you can keep them in the right order. If your fabric is slightly less than this width, divide it equally and so make the hanging slightly narrower. Reduce the width of the "torii" block to the same measurement (most easily done on a photocopier). Mark out the 36 in/91.5 cm length on the panels but do not cut to size yet as the horizontal piecing may cause a slight run up on the length. Cut pieces of wadding to match.

2 From the deep red fabric, cut 12 strips 1 in/2.5 cm wide across the full width of the cloth. Put aside for the binding. From this fabric also cut five hanging sleeves, each 9½ x 8 in/ 24 x 20 cm. The remaining fabrics will be cut as they are needed during the making of the panels.

STITCHING
Preparation

1 Lay the panels of furnishing fabric right side down and place a piece of wadding on each. Pin, then baste lengthwise in three rows, without knots, so that the thread is easy to remove.

2 Make five tracings or photocopies of the "torii" block (on page 97). Divide into four parts as shown in diagram 1. These do not have seam allowances. Note that the blocks are stitched following the drawn lines but the fabrics are placed on the plain side of the paper. Add the numbers to the master block.

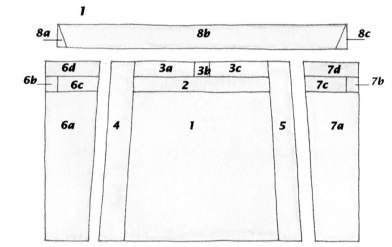

Working the foundation pieced blocks

1 Choose two fabrics, one for the "torii" and one for the background, which you may like to think of as sky. Begin with the central part of the block. Place a piece of background (sky) fabric over the large area **1** on the plain (non-marked) side of the paper. Hold up to the light if wished, to check the fabric covers the whole of area **1** with at least ¼ in/0.75 cm extra all round for seam allowances. Pin, then baste (diagram 2).

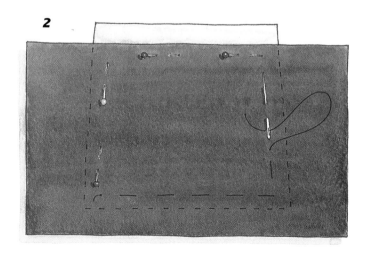

6b

8a

6a

6c

6d

4

2

3a

8b

1

3b

3c

5

7a

7c

7d

7b

8c

2 Place a strip of "torii" fabric, right sides together, along the top edge of the background fabric (to become piece **2**) also with sufficient for seam allowances and pin (diagram 3). Turn the paper over and stitch along the drawn seam, starting ¼ in/ 0.75 cm before the drawn line and continuing the same amount beyond it (diagram 4). Turn back to the fabric side and flip the "torii" fabric right side up. Lightly press with a dry iron. Trim excess from seam allowance below to leave ¼ in/0.75 cm seam allowance.

3

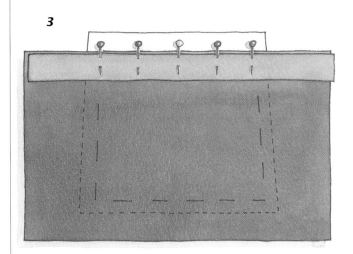

4

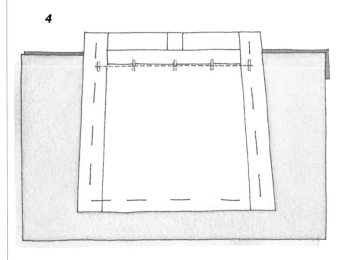

3 Join a 1 in/2.5 cm wide strip of "torii" fabric between two strips of background (**3a, b, c**) and press. Place this right side down with the insert centred on the previous "torii" strip, pin (diagram 5), then turn to the stitching side and stitch. As before, turn back to flip the latest strip right side up and press. Again trim excess from turnings below.

5

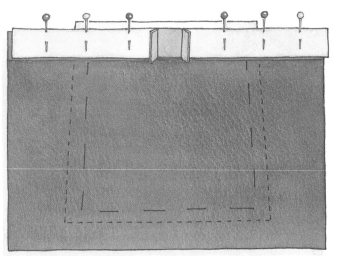

4 Add a strip of "torii" fabric to each side of the centre (**4** and **5**) as shown in diagram 6. Notice that these strips are tapered and when placing them be sure the strips are wide enough for the wider end plus enough for seam allowances. After pressing, trim all three sides to include ¼ in/0.75 cm seam allowance ready for stitching to the next units.

6

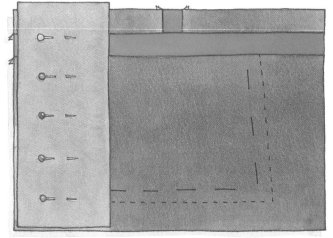

5 In a similar way, work the two side units. Place **6a** first, just as piece **1** on the centre section. Piece a scrap of background (**6b**) to a strip of "torii" fabric (**6c**) before attaching to the top edge, then add strip **6d** to the top. Be sure to stitch on the lines (**6 a-d**). Repeat to make the second side unit (**7 a-d**) as shown in diagram 7. Trim to include ¼ in/0.75 cm seam allowances on all sides.

7

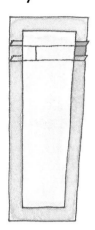 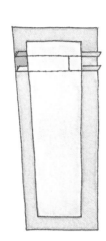

6 Work the top unit by placing "torii" fabric (**8b**) over the whole strip and piecing tiny triangles of background on both ends (**8a, c**) as shown in diagram 8. Trim to include ¼ in/0.75 cm seam allowances on all sides.

8

7 Join the side units to the centre, taking ¼ in/0.75 cm turnings and press. Add the top unit and press. Tear away the paper foundations. Repeat to work a total of five blocks.

COMPLETING THE HANGING

1 If possible pin the panels, in the correct order for the printed design on the backing but with wadding side facing you, on a design wall. If you don't have one of these, each panel can be pegged or pinned to a wire coathanger and hung from a picture rail. Decide where the blocks will be on each one. Remember that, although you want a balanced arrangement, this does not have to be symmetrical. Pin temporarily in place.

2 Check the block is straight before basting in position on the panel along the short sides within the turnings.

3 Work strip piecing above and below the basted blocks to fill the rest of each panel. To speed the work, I suggest choosing a group of fabrics for each panel and cutting a few strips from each of them of varying widths. Include some tapered strips as their angles add more interest to the finished piece. Angled strips need to be slightly longer, so that when flipped right side up they cover the width of the panel completely.

4 Place the first strip, right side down, at either the top or the bottom edge of the block on the strip. Machine-stitch through all layers (diagram 9). Flip the strip right side up and lightly press. Place a few pins at right angles along the sides before putting the next strip right side down on top and repeating the process. Continue until all the panels are filled.

9

5 Measure the length of the panels and re-mark the 36 in/ 91.5 cm length if necessary. Baste along the short ends of the panels within the seam allowance. Trim away excess wadding and backing from all panels.

6 Join the binding strips and use to bind the panels, turn over and blind-hem to finish ¼ in/0.75 cm wide.

7 Add a hanging sleeve to the back of each panel, then thread onto the hanging pole.

PIONEER BLANKETS

Quiltmaking has come full circle with the current use of homespuns, double-brushed flannels and wools. There has been a return to simple quilts made for everyday use in place of quilts that will become treasured heirlooms. The nature of these types of fabric does not allow for intricate piecing or for fine hand-quilting, so they are ideal for the quilter in a hurry. The fabric is softer, thicker and more loosely woven than the cottons to which we have more recently become accustomed. Since the fabrics are thicker, it is advisable to use a very fine wadding. Flannels and wools are nevertheless fun to work with and produce wonderfully cosy quilts to snuggle up in on those cold winter days. The quilts in this section all take their inspiration from the blankets used and traded by the American pioneers.

−ANNE WALKER

PIONEER PATCHES

The early pioneers found themselves making quilts that were warm, quick and easy, as they set off in search of new lands and a new life. Guidebooks for the times suggested that settlers should take with them a good number of quilts to sustain them throughout their journey. Many of the pioneers experienced hard times on their travels; their quilts were used for bedding, shelter and often burial wraps. These simple, hard-wearing quilts were made from left-over suiting, tailors' samples or, in fact, anything that they could lay their hands on. This quilt tries to achieve the look of an early pioneer's quilt. I used sample fabric swatches from a department store that were being thrown out at the end of a season and made the quilt in about eight hours. I hand-quilted but machine-quilting would take another two hours or so. You could use swatches or any fabric that you may have on hand. If you need to purchase the fabric, the variety will have to be reduced in order to keep the cost realistic but a pleasing result can still be achieved.

It makes a cosy lap quilt or sofa throw.

Quilt size: 48 x 60 in/ 120 x 150 cm

MATERIALS

Suiting/wool blends: 11 different fabrics, ⅓ yard / 30 cm each, 45 in/115 cm wide

Backing: 3 yards/2.7 metres, 45 in/115 cm wide

Binding: ½ yard/50 cm, 45 in/115 cm wide

Wadding: fine, 52 x 64 in/130 x 160 cm

Quilting thread: soft cotton embroidery thread

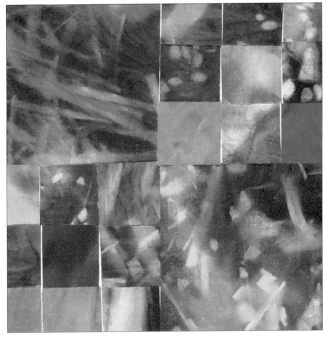

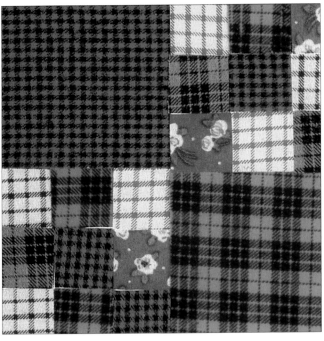

ALTERNATIVE COLOUR SCHEMES

These four colourways feature different types of fabric and a variety of colour ranges and designs to show how dramatically you can alter the overall look. Choose a monochromatic theme and use a large selection of tones in one colourway. This one is "red" but uses fabric from pink to burgundy. Alternatively, use the design to show off a collection of hand-dyed fabrics in all sorts of colours and designs. The design lends itself to warm cosy flannels as in the original: this alternative interpretation uses some patterned fabrics. For an alternative plain and simple design, choose strong Amish colours to give a characteristically striking colour scheme.

CUTTING

1 If you are using samples or scraps, cut 64 squares measuring $6\frac{1}{2}$ in/16.5 cm and 144 squares measuring $2\frac{1}{2}$ in/6.5 cm. Alternatively from each of the 11 fabrics, cut one $6\frac{1}{2}$ in/ 16.5 cm strip and sub-cut into squares and one $2\frac{1}{2}$ in/6.5 cm strip and sub-cut into squares.

2 Cut the backing fabric in half and stitch together to form a rectangle, 54 x 90 in/130 x 230 cm. From this cut a rectangle, 52 x 64 in/130 x 160 cm.

3 Cut the binding fabric into strips $2\frac{1}{2}$ in/7 cm wide.

STITCHING

1 Lay out a set of nine small squares to form a "Nine-patch": try to ensure that no two pieces of fabric are the same. Lay another 15 sets down on top to form a stack of "Nine-patches" and number each stack (diagram 1).

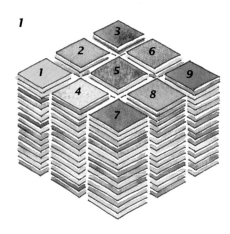

2 Flip square **2** onto square **1**, right sides together, and stitch with an exact $\frac{1}{4}$ in/0.75 cm seam. Continue to chain-piece all the **2**s to the **1**s. Do not cut apart (diagram 2).

> **When working with wools, clean the lint from your sewing machine regularly.**

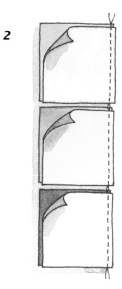

3 Chain-piece all the **3**s to the **2**s (diagram 3). Cut apart and press the seams towards the centre square. Lay down in position again.

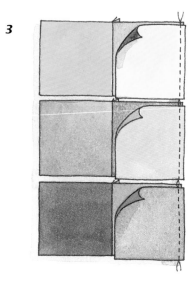

4 Chain-piece **4**, **5** and **6** in the same way. Cut apart and press towards the outside squares. Lay down in position.

5 Chain-piece **7**, **8** and **9** in the same way. Cut apart and press towards the centre square. Lay down in position.

6 Join the horizontal rows to complete the "Nine-patch" blocks. Press the seams in one direction.

7 Lay out the plain squares and the "Nine-patches" as shown in the quilt plan. Try to avoid the same fabrics touching.

8 Piece each row horizontally. Press the seams on odd rows to the left and even rows to the right. Stitch the rows together, matching seams where appropriate. Press all these seams in one direction.

FINISHING THE QUILT

1 Layer the backing, wadding and quilt top. Pin and baste in a grid, starting from the centre.

2 Quilt in a pattern of your choice. I have quilted by hand in a diagonal pattern through the centre of the squares using soft embroidery cotton and a "big stitch" (see "Utility quilting" on page 63). Machine-quilting the same design or tying the quilt would both work well and be quicker.

3 When the quilting is completed, trim excess backing and wadding, stitch the binding strips together to the length required and use to bind the quilt with a doublefold binding.

STAR AND STRIPES

As the pioneers moved westwards, they settled in lands that had hitherto been the domain of the Native American. Early trappers and mountain men made contact with the tribes, and trade that had started with the Hudson Bay Company flourished. With the demise of the buffalo, the blankets took on great importance, replacing the buffalo robes worn on ceremonial occasions by the Native American. The simplest blanket was one with bands of colour at each end. The blankets were double woven and often contained reversed colours. This simple reversible top quilt reflects these ideas and can be made except for the hand-quilting in about four hours.

Quilt size: 45 x 60 in/115 x 152 cm

MATERIALS

All fabrics used in the quilt are 45 in/115 cm wide.

Two main plain-coloured soft flannel fabrics: 1½ yards/1.5 metres each

Three contrasting plain-coloured soft flannel fabrics for the bands: ⅓ yard/30 cm each
Wadding: fine, 45 x 70 in/115 x 180 cm
Binding: ½ yard/50 cm, 45 in/115 cm wide
Quilting thread: soft embroidery cotton

CUTTING

1 From each of the main fabrics, cut one 45 x 40½ in/ 115 x 104 cm rectangle and two 45 x 4 in/115 x 10.5 cm strips.

2 From each of the contrasting fabrics, cut four 45 x 2½ in/ 115 x 7.5 cm strips.

3 From the wadding, cut one 45 x 40½ in/115 x 104 cm rectangle; six 45 x 2½ in/115 x 7.5 cm strips and two 45 x 4 in/115 x 10.5 cm strips.

4 Cut the binding fabric into strips 2½ in/7 cm wide.

STITCHING

1 Take the large rectangles of flannel and wadding and make up a sandwich with the wadding in the middle and the flannels right sides out. Pin and baste in a grid working from the centre out.

2 Using a zigzag stitch, stitch round the outside to close all four sides of the rectangle.

3 Take two strips of the first contrast fabric. Lay one underneath the long edge of the rectangle, right sides together and raw edges aligned, and one on top of the long edge, right sides together and raw edges aligned. On the top of this lay a strip of 2½ in/7.5 cm wadding. Pin together (diagram 1).

1

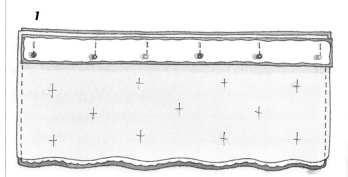

4 Stitch through all layers with an exact ¼ in/0.75cm seam allowance. Neaten the raw edge of the seam with a zigzag stitch (diagram 2).

2

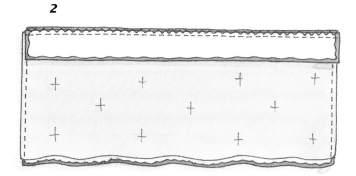

5 Flip the strips upwards to sandwich the wadding between the two strips. Pin together (diagram 3) and neaten the raw edge with a zigzag stitch.

3

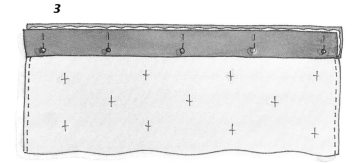

6 Take two of the second contrasting fabric strips and another strip of wadding and apply to the edge of the first strip, flipping and stitching as before (diagram 4). Repeat for the third contrasting fabric strip.

4

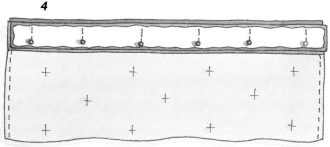

7 Take one strip of each of the main fabrics and the 4 in/ 10.5 cm wide wadding strip and stitch in the same manner to the third contrasting strip.

8 Following the quilt plan, repeat all these steps to complete the other end of the quilt to match.

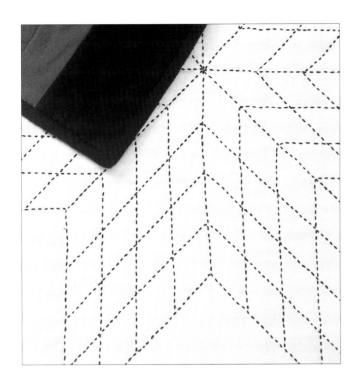

❝ The fabric sandwich for the central portion has already been tacked in a grid, so is now ready to quilt. ❞

FINISHING THE QUILT

1 Quilt in the pattern of your choice. I quilted a radiant star motif with soft embroidery cotton using a "big stitch". The star is made up of eight diamonds broken down into smaller diamonds (diagram 5).

2 When the quilting is completed, stitch the binding strips together to make the length required and use to bind the quilt with a doublefold binding.

5

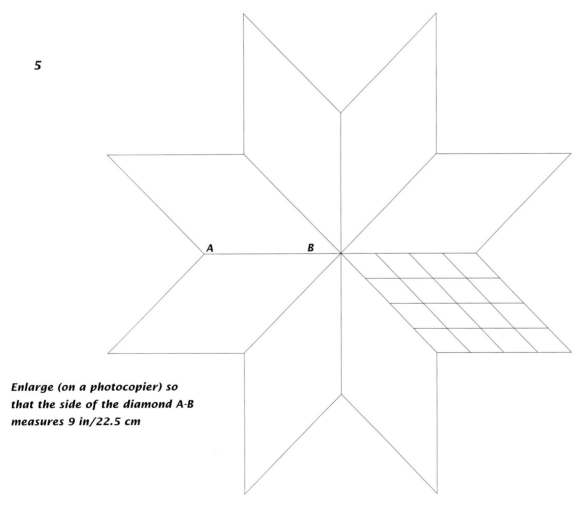

A   B

Enlarge (on a photocopier) so that the side of the diamond A-B measures 9 in/22.5 cm

NAVAJO

Navajo weavers often wove designs similar in look to Florentine or bargello tapestry. Trade blanket manufacturers took this design idea and created similar all-over woven designs. This wool quilt takes the idea and creates a bargello-style lap quilt with a Navajo feel, which can be made in about 18 hours.

Quilt size: 48 x 66 in/114 x 144 cm

MATERIALS

Plain wool: six different colours, ½ yard /50 cm each, 60 in/150 cm wide

Binding: ½ yard/50 cm, 60 in/150 cm wide

Backing: 52 x 70 in/124 x 154 cm. (I used 45 in/ 115 cm wide flannel. Take 4 yards/3.1 metres, cut and join and cut out a rectangle of the required size.)

Wadding: fine, 52 x 70 in/124 x 154 cm

CUTTING

1 From each of the six plain wool fabrics, cut three strips 6 in/13.5 cm wide.

2 Cut the binding fabric into strips 2½ in/7 cm wide.

STITCHING

1 Lay out one strip from each of the six fabrics in the order that you like best.

2 Stitch in three sets of six, using an accurate ¼ in/0.75 cm seam (diagram 1).

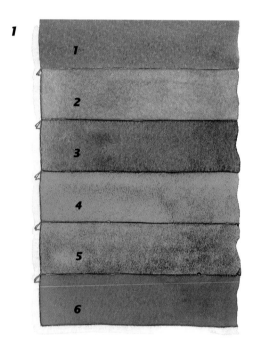

3 Fold a set of stitched strips in half, right sides together and with the fold towards you, then sub-cut at right angles to the seam in 3 in/7.5 cm strips (diagram 2).

4 Join two strips end to end (diagram 3). Continue to join strips until you have 19 strips, 12 units long.

5 Set three of these strips to one side. Join the ends of each of the remaining 16 strips until you have 16 complete circles (diagram 4).

6 Unpick the circles to form new strips, following the chart below. The first strip will have fabric **4** at the top and fabric **3** at the bottom. Lay out the strips in the order shown on the quilt plan, starting from the left.

	Top fabric	Bottom fabric
Row 1	4	3
Row 2	5	4
Row 3	6	5
Row 4	1	6 (this is one of the reserved strips)
Row 5	6	5
Row 6	5	4
Row 7	4	3
Row 8	5	4
Row 9	6	5
Row 10	1	6 (this is the second reserved strip)
Row 11	6	5
Row 12	5	4
Row 13	4	3
Row 14	5	4
Row 15	6	5
Row 16	1	6 (this is the last of the reserved strips)
Row 17	6	5
Row 18	5	4
Row 19	4	3

7 Press odd rows with the seams facing up and even rows with the seams facing down.

8 Join all the rows in order, starting from the left and matching all horizontal seams as you go. Press in one direction.

FINISHING THE QUILT

1 Layer the backing, wadding and quilt top. Pin and baste the layers together in a grid, starting from the centre and working outwards.

2 Quilt in the pattern of your choice. I have machine-quilted in-the-ditch but tying would also give a nice appearance.

3 When the quilting is completed, stitch the binding strips together to the length required and use to bind the quilt with a doublefold binding.

COVERED FIRE

J. Capps and Son made a name for themselves with their trade blankets featuring many-banded designs, which had patterns woven into the stripes. "Buffalo Bill" Cody described wrapping up in a Capps blanket as a realization of "a dream of the far prairie and a covered fire". This quilt uses the banded design idea and is constructed using 60 in/150 cm wide felted wool. It can be made in about 24 hours. This is the traditional size, as it was the maximum size that could be woven on the looms, and so makes a perfect topper for a single bed.

◆

Quilt size: 60 x 72 in/150 x 180 cm

MATERIALS

Fabric 1: ½ yard/50 cm, 60 in/150 cm wide
Fabric 2: ½ yard/50 cm, 60 in/150 cm wide
Fabric 3: ¾ yard/70 cm, 60 in/150 cm wide
Fabric 4: ½ yard/50 cm, 60 in/150 cm wide
Fabric 5: ⅜ yard/35 cm, 60 in/150 cm wide
Fabric 6: ¼ yard/25 cm, 60 in/150 cm wide
Fabric 7: ⅞ yard/75 cm, 60 in/150 cm wide

Binding: flannel, ½ yard/50 cm, 45 in/115 cm wide
Backing: 64 x 76 in/160 x 190 cm (I used 45 in/115 cm wide flannel, I therefore had 4¼ yards/3.8 metres, which I cut and joined to create the required size.)
Wadding: fine, 64 x 76 in/160 x 190 cm

CUTTING

1 From fabric **1**, cut one strip $6\frac{1}{2}$ in/16.5cm wide and two strips $3\frac{1}{2}$ in/9 cm wide, sub-cut into $6\frac{1}{2}$ in/16.5 cm rectangles.

2 From fabric **2**, cut two strips $3\frac{1}{2}$ in/9 cm wide. Cut three more strips $3\frac{1}{2}$ in/9 cm, sub-cut to get 18 rectangles $6\frac{1}{2}$ in/16.5 cm long and four squares measuring $3\frac{1}{2}$ in/9 cm.

3 From fabric **3**, cut four strips $3\frac{1}{2}$ in/9 cm wide. Cut two more strips $3\frac{1}{2}$ in/9 cm wide, sub-cut to get eight rectangles $6\frac{1}{2}$ in/16.5 cm long and four squares measuring $3\frac{1}{2}$ in/9 cm.

4 From fabric **4**, cut four strips $3\frac{1}{2}$ in/9 cm wide, sub-cut to get four squares $3\frac{1}{2}$ in/9 cm, six rectangles $18\frac{1}{2}$ in/43.5 cm long and four rectangles $15\frac{1}{2}$ in/36.5 cm long.

5 From fabric **5**, cut three strips $3\frac{1}{2}$ in/9 cm wide, sub-cut to get ten rectangles $12\frac{1}{2}$ in/29.5 cm long.

6 From fabric **6**, cut two strips $3\frac{1}{2}$ in/9 cm wide, sub-cut to get ten rectangles $6\frac{1}{2}$ in/16.5 cm long.

7 From fabric **7**, cut eight strips $3\frac{1}{2}$ in/9 cm wide, sub-cut to get ten rectangles $6\frac{1}{2}$ in/16.5 cm long, ten rectangles $12\frac{1}{2}$ in/29.5 cm long, six rectangles $18\frac{1}{2}$ in/43.5 cm long, four rectangles $15\frac{1}{2}$ in/36.5 cm long and four squares measuring $3\frac{1}{2}$ in/9 cm.

8 Cut the binding into strips $2\frac{1}{2}$ in/7 cm wide.

STITCHING

1 Consulting the quilt plan at all times, lay out two lots of row **A**. Join the pieces, chain-piecing where possible, using a $\frac{1}{4}$ in/0.75 cm seam allowance, press the seams open to cope with the thickness of the wool.

2 Lay out two lots of row **B**, join and press all the seams open as before. Continue in this manner until you have two rows of **C**, **D**, **E**, **F**, **G** and **H**.

3 Lay out all the rows in the order shown in the quilt plan, including the unpieced rows, and stitch one half from the centre outwards, lining up the seams as you go.

4 Complete the remainder of the quilt to match. Press all the seams open.

FINISHING THE QUILT

1 Layer the backing, wadding and quilt top. Pin and baste in a grid, starting from the centre.

2 Quilt in a pattern of your choice. I have quilted in-the-ditch by machine.

3 When the quilting is completed, stitch the binding strips together to the length required and use to bind the quilt with a doublefold binding.

OREGON CORNHUSK
TEMPLATES

Instructions for using the templates are given on pages 120–121

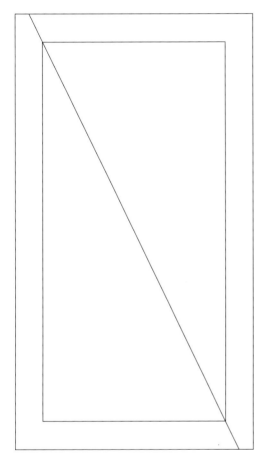

small rectangle, finished size: 5 x 10 cm

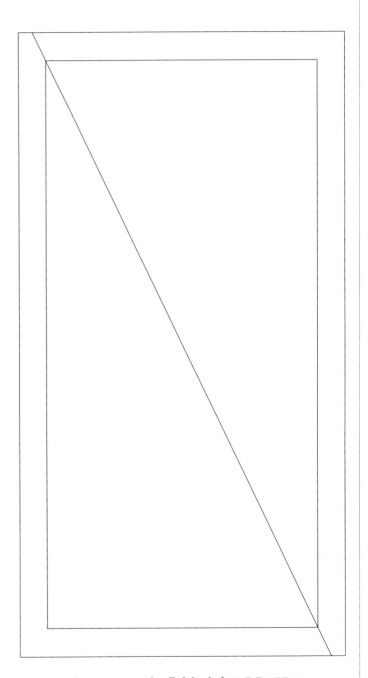

large rectangle, finished size: 7.5 x 15 cm

OREGON CORNHUSK

This single bed quilt has more complicated piecing than the other projects in this section, so will take roughly 30 hours to make. However, the style of the quilt completes the study of trade blankets as a design source. Trade blanket designs were often made up of six or nine elements. These elements translate directly for the quiltmaker into blocks. Native Americans in the plateau region, which includes Oregon, produced bags to carry berries, fish, etc., that they had gathered or hunted. Many of these bags were embellished with geometric designs using cornhusks, hence the name of this quilt. These designs often included a rectangle split into two long thin triangles. These triangles can be produced quickly using the "BiRangle".

Quilt size: 54 x 60 in/135 x 150 cm

MATERIALS

All fabrics used in the quilt top are 45 in/115 cm wide.

Fabric 1: 1 yard/1 metre
Fabric 2: 1 yard/1 metre
Fabric 3: 1 yard/1 metre
Fabric 4: 2 yards/2 metres

Fabric 5: ½ yard/50 cm
Fabric 6: 1 yard/1 metre
Backing: 58 x 64 in/140 x160 cm
Wadding: fine, 58 x 64 in/140 x 160 cm
Binding: ½ yard/50 cm, 45 in/115 cm wide

As the "BiRangle" is currently only made with imperial measurements, instructions at the point of making the "bias rectangles" are given only in inches. For those of you working in metric, there are templates and separate instructions for their use.

CUTTING

1 From fabric **1**, cut five $4\frac{1}{2}$ in/11.5 cm strips; sub-cut to get nine squares, $4\frac{1}{2}$ in/11.5 cm wide and 36 rectangles, $3\frac{1}{2}$ x $4\frac{1}{2}$ in/9 x 11.5 cm. Trim down the remainder to $2\frac{1}{2}$ in/ 7.5 cm and cut one rectangle, $12\frac{1}{2}$ in/31.5 cm long. Cut one $12\frac{1}{2}$ in/31.5 cm strip and sub-cut into 17 rectangles, $12\frac{1}{2}$ x $2\frac{1}{2}$ in/31.5 x 7.5 cm.

2 From fabric **4**, cut two $2\frac{1}{2}$ in/7.5 cm strips and sub-cut into 18 rectangles measuring $2\frac{1}{2}$ x $4\frac{1}{2}$ in/7.5 x 11.5 cm.

3 Using the remainder of fabric **4** and fabrics **2**, **3**, and **6**, cut into 18 in/50 cm pieces. These pieces will be for making the bias rectangle units. The "BiRangle" tool comes with complete instructions which I will not repeat here. You will need to make eight different units as shown in diagram 1.

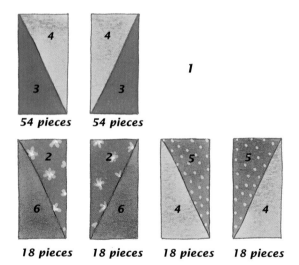

54 pieces   **54 pieces**   *1*

18 pieces   **18 pieces**   **18 pieces**   **18 pieces**

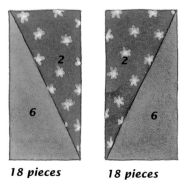

18 pieces   **18 pieces**

4 Lay fabrics **3** and **4** on top of each other with folds to the left and selvages to the right (diagram 2).

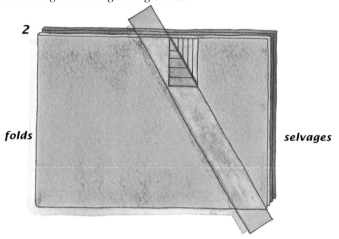

2

folds   *selvages*

5 Set up for the "BiRangle" as shown in diagram 2 and use the instructions with the tool to cut both sets of half yards/metres into 3 in strips. Set aside carefully.

6 Use the "BiRangle" similarly for fabrics **4** and **5**. Cut the set into 3 in strips and set aside carefully. Fabrics **2** and **6** will be cut at a later stage.

STITCHING

1 Working with fabrics **3** and **4**, stitch the strips in matching pairs, right sides together, using an exact $\frac{1}{4}$ in seam. Press carefully. Divide the strips evenly in half.

2 Use one half, right side up, to cut rectangles measuring $2\frac{1}{2}$ x $4\frac{1}{2}$ in using the "BiRangle". You will need 54 pieces.

3 Use the remaining strips and repeat the process, but with the wrong side uppermost, to give the slope of the triangle in the opposite direction. Again you will need 54 pieces.

4 Working with the strips from fabrics **4** and **5**, stitch in matching pairs, right sides together, using an exact $\frac{1}{4}$ in seam. Press carefully. Divide the strips evenly in half.

5 Use one half of the strips with right sides up and cut 18 rectangles measuring $2\frac{1}{2}$ x $4\frac{1}{2}$ in. Use the other half with wrong sides up to cut 18 more rectangles.

Metric

1 If you are working in metric, use the small template (on page 117) for all the above rectangles. Transfer the design onto a piece of card or template plastic. Place the diagonal line of the template on the seam line on the right side for half the set and on the wrong side for the other half.

CUTTING AND STITCHING FABRICS 2 AND 6

1 Set the two half yards/metres of fabric up for using the "BiRangle" as before. Cut three sets of strips 4 in/10.5 cm wide.

2 Stitch in matching pairs, press carefully and divide into two even groups.

3 Using one set, right sides up, cut rectangles measuring 3½ x 6½ in, using either the "BiRangle" or the large template (on page 117) if working in metric. You will need 18 rectangles. Join waste triangles along the bias edge to make up the number. Any waste that is too small can be used later.

4 Using the other set, cut rectangles from the stitched strips with the wrong side up. Again you will need 18 large rectangles.

5 Once you have enough large rectangles, cut the remaining fabric at the same angle but 3 in/8 cm wide. Pair and stitch to make small rectangles: 18 with right side facing and 18 with wrong side facing. Waste triangles can be used to complete the number if necessary.

3

COMPLETING THE BLOCKS

1 Lay out the blocks as in diagram 3. Stitch the pieces in vertical rows, chain-piecing where it will help.

2 Stitch these rows together to form the block. Repeat until you have nine blocks.

FINISHING THE QUILT

1 Lay out the quilt blocks as the quilt plan and stitch together like a large "Nine-patch".

2 Layer the backing, wadding and quilt top, pin and baste in a grid from the centre out.

3 Quilt in a pattern of your choice. I machine-quilted in-the-ditch, emphasizing the diamonds that are produced when the blocks are joined.

4 When the quilting is completed, join the binding strips as required and use to bind the quilt with doublefold binding.

NIGHT and DAY

Save time in making quilts by not shopping for fabrics but dyeing your own using 100% cotton, several jam or coffee jars and a tin of Dylon cold water dye. It's a simple process to achieve fabrics which have many colour blotches, mottled areas, crinkles and dye creases. Dyeing becomes more time consuming if an overall even colour is required owing to the amount of stirring needed! Jam it in a jar for an instant effect! The American quilter, Vimala McClure, calls it "fabric pickling". I've used these colour variations to portray different aspects of the countryside, whether it's the approaching night, autumn leaves or sunlit water.

Three quilts are made using dyed fabric, another is made from Kunin acrylic felt, which is hand washable and does not shrink or fray, and the fifth is pieced with a combination of bought and hand-dyed fabrics. All quilts, apart from the cot quilt, have backings which have also been dyed, but a plain or print fabric could be used instead.

You can use worn cotton sheets to cut down the cost of quilting by dyeing the best pieces. Fabric can be bought that is already prepared for dyeing but I find that if fabric is machine washed first with soap powder, there are no problems. Some shrinkage can occur and quantities given for each project allow extra for this. Hand-dyed fabric is becoming easier to buy but is much more expensive than doing it yourself.

– CAROL DOWSETT

SQUARE ON SQUARE

This single bed quilt, based on a 12 in/30 cm block, took approximately 14 hours to complete. Each block is made from a centre square of star fabric and four triangles which are cut from two squares. Some triangles and the backing fabric are dyed as one piece and cut after rinsing, washing and drying the fabric. If you don't wish to dye your own fabric, there are now many designer dyed fabrics available. The quilt can be made larger or smaller by altering the number of blocks and the setting.

Quilt size: 57½ x 69½ in/145 x 175 cm

MATERIALS

For backing and 40 triangles: pre-washed white 100% cotton fabric, 3 yards/2.8 metres, 60 in/150 cm wide
Cold water dye: 1 tin Dylon A30 Turquoise Saga
Small bucket or watertight bin
Salt
Cold Fix: 1 packet (15 g)

Dark blue star print fabric: 2 yards/1.9 metres, 45 in/115 cm wide
Cotton print fabric: 5 fat quarters in different reds
Wadding: 2 oz, 60 x 72 in/155 x 185 cm
Clear nylon thread for machine-quilting
Mercerized cotton for tie quilting

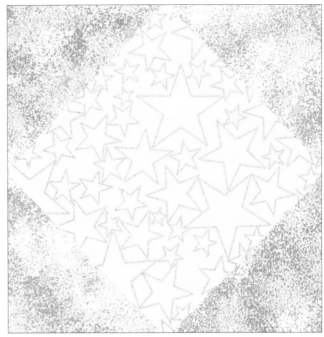

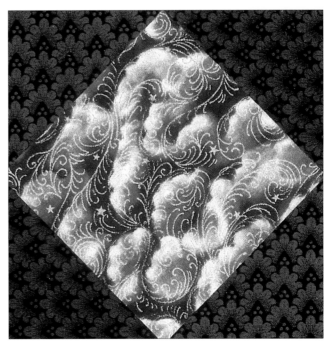

ALTERNATIVE COLOUR SCHEMES

By altering the style and colouring of the fabrics, this quilt changes mood and appeal. The jungle print set in plain yellow makes a great design for a child's bed, while the two gold star fabrics are more suitable for a teenager. Two colourways of the same print produce a bright and graphic design for a sunny room. Alternatively, two dark blue prints create a sophisticated look for a modern bedroom.

NOTES ABOUT DYEING USING COLD WATER DYES (PROCION DYES)

These dyes are safe to use but, nevertheless, when you are using powdered dye, certain precautions must be taken:

✦ Do not breathe in the dye powder, wear a mask if possible, and have handy a damp cloth to wipe up any spills.

✦ Do not use kitchen utensils you have used for dyeing for any culinary purpose.

✦ Wear rubber gloves and old clothing.

✦ Do not dye fabric near any food or food processing areas.

✦ Cover your work area with plastic sheeting or newspapers.

✦ Dispose of dye liquid in an environmentally safe way.

Basic equipment

✦ jam jars/coffee jars (or similar) with lids;

✦ kitchen scales;

✦ tablespoon;

✦ stick for stirring;

✦ 2 measuring jugs;

✦ small bucket or watertight wastepaper bin.

For each tin of dye used you will need:

✦ 4 oz/110 g of salt;

✦ 1 packet of Cold Fix.

General instructions

Use hot water from the tap and not boiling water. Allow two hours for the dye process to take place.

1 Soak white 100% cotton fabric in cold water, then squeeze out excess. Squash the damp fabric as tightly as possible into a ball and wrap some rubber bands around it or tie up with plastic string.

2 Mix the dye into 20 fl oz/500 ml hot water, stir until dissolved and pour into a small bucket or watertight bin.

3 Mix 4 oz/110 g salt and the Cold Fix into 20 fl oz/ 500 ml hot water and stir until dissolved. Pour into the dye solution in the bucket and stir well.

4 Put the fabric "ball" in and press down in the dye, with just enough cold water added to cover (if needed) and leave for two hours.

5 Empty out the dye and rinse fabric in warm water until the water runs clear. Wash with soap powder on a gentle machine cycle, dry and iron. Your fabric is now ready to use.

DYEING

1 Dye the white cotton fabric with the turquoise dye, as described above.

CUTTING

1 From the dark blue star print fabric, cut twenty 9 in/23 cm squares (diagram 1).

1

2 From each fat quarter, cut four squares 6⅞ in/17.5 cm, then cut each square in half to make a total of eight triangles (diagram 2).

2

3 From the hand-dyed turquoise fabric, cut twenty 6⅞ in/ 17.5 cm squares, then cut each square in half to make a total of 40 triangles (diagram 3).

4 From the remainder of this fabric, cut a rectangle, 60 x 72 in/155 x 180 cm for the backing (diagram 3).

3

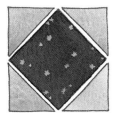

backing

5 For the inner border, cut and join together in a random sequence 1½ in/4 cm wide strips of fabric left from the fat quarters.

6 For the outer border, cut and join together 4 in/10 cm wide strips of fabric across the width of the dark blue star print fabric (diagram 1).

7 Cut the remaining dark blue star print into enough 2 in/ 5 cm wide strips to make a doublefold binding to go round the outer edges of the quilt.

STITCHING

1 Using a set of four triangles in the same fabric, stitch a triangle to each side of one 9 in/23 cm square using a ¼ in/0.75 cm seam (diagram 4). Press the seams open.

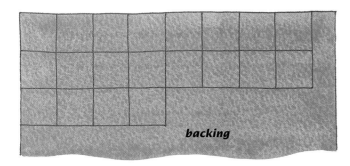

4

2 Following the quilt plan, join the blocks together in rows of four blocks each, alternating the dyed fabric blocks with the others. Stitch the rows together.

ADDING THE BORDERS

1 Measure the quilt top through the centre from side to side. Cut two strips from the red fabric for the inner border to this length. Pin and stitch to the top and bottom of the quilt. Press the seams open.

2 Measure the quilt top through the centre from top to bottom. Cut two red border strips to this length, then pin and stitch to the sides of the quilt. Press the seams open.

3 Repeat this process to add the wider dark blue star print strips for the outer border.

FINISHING THE QUILT

1 Lay out the backing, wadding and top and fasten with safety pins or baste in a grid.

2 Using clear thread on top and regular thread in the bobbin, stitch with a walking foot or even-feed foot "in-the-ditch" along all the straight lines.

3 Machine the double binding all round and either machine or hand stitch to the back.

4 Tie quilt in the centre of the squares with a double thread of mercerized cotton.

AUTUMN LEAVES

Dyeing fabric tightly packed into a small space produces wonderful textures and surprising colour variations. Superimposed on this are hand-printed autumn leaf designs made using a simple printing block from polystyrene or foam. Find a fine-grained piece (such as the tray that vegetables are sold in from supermarkets) or better still, use commercial materials that are sold specifically for printing.

This combination of hand-dyed fabric and hand-printed leaves makes a wall-hanging or table cover that is evocative of a forest with a floor of autumnal foliage. It took roughly 12 hours.

◆

Quilt size: 48½ x 48½ in/123 x 123 cm

MATERIALS

All fabrics used in the quilt are 60 in/150 cm wide.

Fabric marker
Pre-washed white or cream 100% cotton fabric: 2¾ yards/2.5 metres
Backing fabric: 60 x 60in/150 x 150 cm (use 100% cotton and dye if liked, or choose a matching brown)
Cold water dye and Cold Fix: 1 tin Dylon A29 Koala Brown and 1 packet (15 g) of Cold Fix for the quilt top, plus same amount for the backing, if dyeing
Salt and small bucket or watertight bin

Jug and four jam jars
Polystyrene or foam: for making leaf printing shapes
Knitting needle
Fabric paint: Liquitex acrylic paint in jars in various colours (I used burnt umber, metallic copper, metallic pearlescent white, cadmium yellow.)
Paint brush
Silicone or baking parchment paper
Wadding: needle-punched, 54 x 54 in/140 x 140 cm
Clear nylon thread for machine-quilting
Leaf-shaped sequins or buttons: for tie quilting

CUTTING

The fabric strips are cut larger than needed to allow for any shrinkage during the dyeing process. Write a number on the jar and in one corner of each strip to correspond with the jar, using the fabric marker.

1 Cut the following across the width of the white or cream cotton fabric:
+ for jar 1, one strip, 30 in/80 cm wide;
+ for jar 2, one strip, 30 in/80 cm wide;
+ for jar 3, one strip, 22 in/60 cm wide;
+ for jar 4, one strip, 12 in/30 cm wide.

The fabric is sub-cut once it has been dyed (see below).

DYEING

Quilt backing

1 Follow the instructions given on page 126 to dye the backing fabric with one tin of dye and one packet of Cold Fix, if not using purchased brown fabric.

Quilt top

Check before adding any of the salt, fix and dye solution that your jars will be big enough to take the fabric plus the total quantity of liquid by testing with the fabric and water, as listed below, in each jar.

1 Mix 4 oz/110 g salt and one packet of Cold Fix into 20 fl oz/500 ml hot water in a jug and stir until dissolved. Divide this equally between the four jars.

2 Mix the contents of one tin of dye in a measuring jug with a small amount of hot water until all dye has dissolved. Add more hot water to make 20 fl oz/500 ml.

3 Divide this between the four jars as follows, stirring the liquid well in each jar:
+ into jar 1 put 4 fl oz/100 ml;
+ into jar 2 put 6 fl oz/150 ml;
+ into jar 3 put 8 fl oz/200 ml;
+ into jar 4 put 2 fl oz/50 ml.

4 Add the numbered damp cut fabrics to the corresponding jars, pressing them down as tightly as possible with a stick or a spoon. Make sure the fabric in each jar has been covered by the solution – even if only just! Press the fabric down further rather than add more water.

5 Leave for two hours, turning each jar three or four times during this time to allow the dye to penetrate different parts of the fabric.

6 Empty the jars and rinse the fabric until the water runs clear. Finish by washing (with soap powder) on a cool cycle in the washing machine. Dry and iron.

CUTTING

1 From fabric **1**, cut three **a** squares 8½ in/21.5 cm and two **b** strips 8½ x 24½ in/21.5 x 61.5 cm.

2 From fabric **2**, cut two **c** strips 8½ x 24½ in/21.5 x 61.5 cm and one **d** strip 8½ x 40½ in/21.5 x 101.5 cm.

3 From fabric **3**, cut one **e** strip 8½ x 40½ in/21.5 x 101.5 cm and two **f** strips 4½ x 40½ in/11.5 x 101.5 cm.

4 From fabric **4**, cut two **g** strips 4½ x 48½ in/ 11.5x 121.5 cm.

5 Cut the pieces of fabric left into strips 2 in/5 cm wide for the binding.

STITCHING

1 Stitch the dyed strips together as shown in diagram 1. This is a "Courthouse Steps" variation of "Log Cabin" patchwork. Use a ¼ in/0.75 cm seam and press all seams open.

1

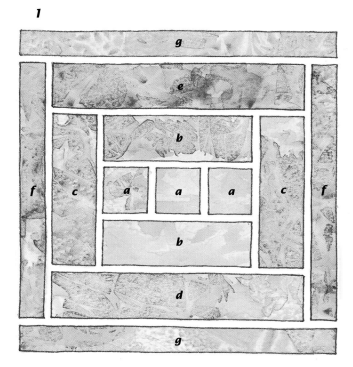

2

PRINTING

1 Trace the leaf shape patterns (diagram 2) and cut out from the polystyrene or foam with scissors. Mark on leaf veins with a knitting needle.

2 Attach a piece of masking tape to the back of each leaf block to make a handle.

3 Put the paint directly onto the print block using a large brush, combine two colours and try printing on spare fabric first. When you have perfected your technique, print the leaves in groups, across any seam lines, making each a slightly different colour. Allow the paint to dry and iron on a hot setting using silicone or baking parchment paper to protect the fabric.

FINISHING THE QUILT

1 Lay out the backing, wadding and top and fasten with safety pins or baste in a grid system.

2 Using clear thread on top and regular thread in the bobbin, stitch "in-the-ditch" along all the straight lines. Trim the excess wadding and backing level with the quilt top.

3 Stitch the binding strips together to make the length required and use to bind the quilt with a doublefold binding.

4 Tie-quilt with leaf-shaped sequins or buttons at random positions all over the quilt.

SHIMMERING WATER

Using a combination of dyeing and fabric painting, this wall-hanging shows a scene of thick bulrushes beside a sunlit lake. It took about 10 hours. To give more of a shimmer to the golden water, strips of fraying metallic fabrics are stitched with "big stitch" quilting. The bulrushes are printed on and fraying fabrics are stitched down in between to add a feeling of depth to the picture.

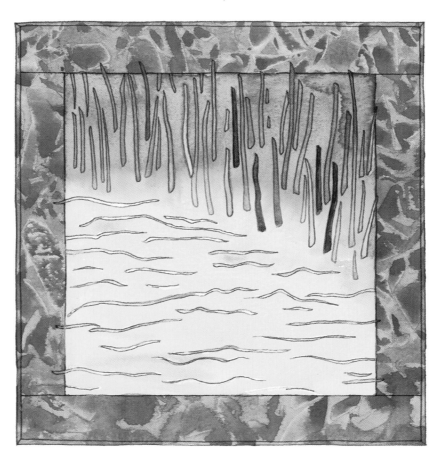

Quilt size: 36 x 36 in/90 x 90 cm

MATERIALS

Pre-washed white 100% cotton fabric: 2.5 yards/ 2.3 metres, 60 in/150 cm wide

Cold water dye: 1 tin Dylon A22 Sahara Sun; 1 tin Dylon A25 Bronze Rose

Salt

Cold Fix: 2 packets (15 g each)

2 measuring jugs and stirring stick

Plastic sheeting

1½ in/4 cm household paint brush

Small bucket or watertight bin

Small strips of polystyrene or foam: for printing

Fabric paints: Liquitex acrylic in jars in various colours (I used burnt umber, pearlescent white and metallic copper.)

Silicone or baking parchment paper

Wadding: needle-punched, 40 x 40 in/100 x 100 cm

Small pieces of sheer, metallic and glitzy fabrics

Embroidery thread: fine coton à broder to match the colour range used in the hanging

CUTTING

1 Cut a 32 in/80 cm square from one corner of the fabric for the quilt top (diagram 1) and leave the cutting of the rest until it has been dyed.

PAINTING AND DYEING

Painting the water scene

1 Dissolve the Sahara Sun dye into 5 fl oz/150 ml of hot water.

2 Mix 4 oz/110 g salt and one packet of Cold Fix into 10 fl oz/300 ml hot water, then combine in a jug with the dye mixture.

3 Mix the Bronze Rose separately, using the same recipe and put into a separate jug – do not combine the two colours.

4 Dampen the 32 in/80 cm square of fabric, then place on the plastic sheeting and smooth out.

5 Dip the paint brush into the yellow dye and paint the bottom half of the water scene as shown on the quilt plan. Paint more dye onto some areas to alter the depth of colour.

6 With the bronze colour and a clean brush, paint the top half of the fabric, letting the two colours run into each other and again going over some areas so that they will be a stronger shade. Work as quickly as possible – it doesn't matter how wet the fabric becomes!

7 Place a piece of plastic on top (to aid "curing") and leave at least two hours and preferably overnight, then rinse, wash, dry and iron.

Dyeing the borders and backing

1 As soon as you have finished dye painting, dampen the remaining fabric and squash it into a small bucket or watertight bin.

2 Pour the remaining bronze rose dye mixture over it, slowly and directly onto the fabric, moving the fabric around with a stick or a gloved hand to make sure the dye gets to most areas. Push tightly into a ball.

3 Pour on the remaining Sahara Sun dye mixture slowly as before. Scrunch the ball tightly down to soak up all the dye. If you feel that there is not enough liquid add a little cold water. Leave for two hours, then rinse, wash, dry and iron.

CUTTING

1 Trim the water scene to a square 28½ in/71.5 cm.

2 From the dyed fabric, cut two strips for the sides, 4¼ x 28½ in/10.75 x 71.5 cm; two strips for the top and bottom, 4¼ x 36 in/10.75 x 90 cm (diagram 1).

1

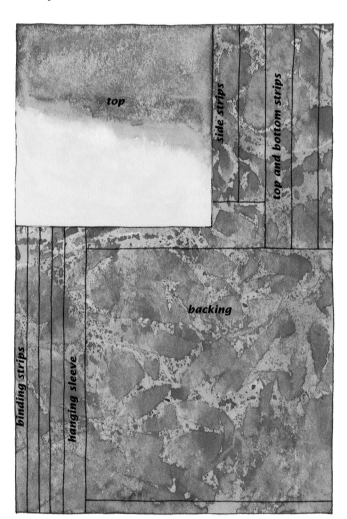

3 For the backing, cut a 40 in/100 cm square (diagram 1).

4 For the doublefold binding, cut strips 2 in/5 cm wide and long enough when joined to go all around the hanging (diagram 1).

5 For the hanging sleeve, cut a strip 7½ x 36 in/19 x 90 cm.

STITCHING AND PRINTING

1 Stitch on the side strips first, matching centres, and press the seams towards the outer edges.

2 Stitch on the top and bottom strips and press the seams as before.

3 Trace off the "bulrush" printing shape patterns (diagram 2) and cut these out from the polystyrene or foam.

4 Put fabric paint onto the shapes and print over the top half of the water scene – try this out first onto spare dyed fabric to test the colours and the technique (see page 131 for more information). Combine paint colours. Use the edges and flat surface of the print blocks to vary the shapes, and lean some at different angles into the side borders (see quilt plan). Use the white metallic paint on a brush to make areas of shimmer on the water. Let the paint dry and iron, using silicone or baking parchment paper to protect the fabric surface.

FINISHING THE QUILT

1 Layer the backing, wadding and quilt top and use safety pins or baste into a grid system.

2 Cut narrow strips of sheer, metallic and glitzy fabrics on the bias (this slows down the fraying), place either on top or to one side of the printed shapes and stitch with "big stitch" quilting (see "Utility quilting" page 63) through the centre of each. Quilt some lines without fabric strips. Use these techniques for the shimmering water also.

3 Stitch on the 2 in/5 cm doublefold binding and attach a hanging sleeve.

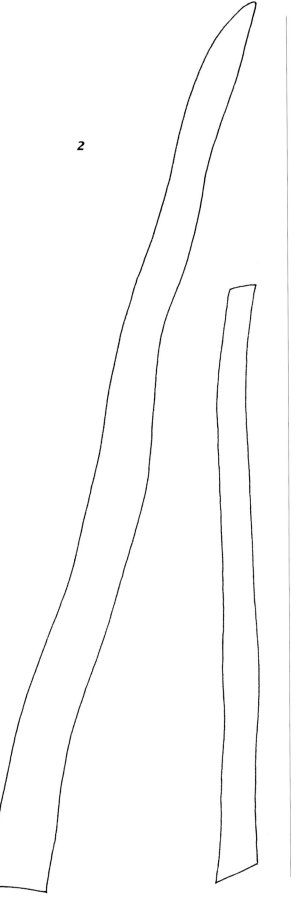

2

DUSK

To perfect a fabric that has glimpses of differing blues from palest to darkest, that evokes the approaching night sky, is surprisingly simple to achieve using cold water dyes! This technique uses tightly scrunched-up fabric, tied into a ball, then immersed in just enough dye solution to cover it. The very centre of this ball will absorb only a little dye liquid and other areas more. The fabric is dyed before it is cut for the quilt. This quilt is based on a 12 in/30 cm block and is designed as a single bed quilt. By altering the number of blocks and keeping the same width edge strips, any size quilt can be made. This size took about 20 hours.

Quilt size: 60 x 84 in/150 x 210 cm

MATERIALS

Pre-washed white 100% cotton fabric: 4 yards/ 3.6 metres, 60 in/150 cm wide
Rubber bands or plastic string
Cold water dye: 1 tin of Dylon A28 Riviera Blue; 1 tin of Dylon Al8 Nasturtium
2 small buckets or watertight bins
Salt
Cold Fix: 2 packets (15 g each)
Backing: 100% cotton, 2½ yards/2.3 metres, 90 in/

230 cm wide (If you wish to dye this fabric, use 1 tin of Dylon A28 Riviera Blue and 1 packet of Cold Fix and use the general dyeing instructions given on page 126)
Wadding: cotton, 64 x 88 in/160 x 220 cm ("Warm and Natural" is recommended)
Machine-quilting thread in blue and orange
Thin card to make star template
Kunin felt: dark blue, 18 in/50 cm, 36 in/90 cm wide
Freezer paper

DYEING

Cut the white cotton fabric in half crosswise to make two pieces, 2 yards/1.8 metres long. Dye one blue and the other orange, as described below.

1 Dampen the pieces of fabric, then squash each into a tight ball. Tie around with rubber bands or plastic string.

2 Mix the contents of each tin of dye into 20 fl oz/500 ml of hot water and pour each into a small bucket. Mix 4 oz/110 g salt and one packet of Cold Fix into 20 fl oz/500 ml of hot water. Add to one of the buckets and stir well. Repeat for the second bucket.

3 Add one ball of fabric to each bucket and push it around and under the dye to get it saturated with the solution. Add a little more cold water if necessary. Leave for two hours, then rinse, wash, dry and iron.

1

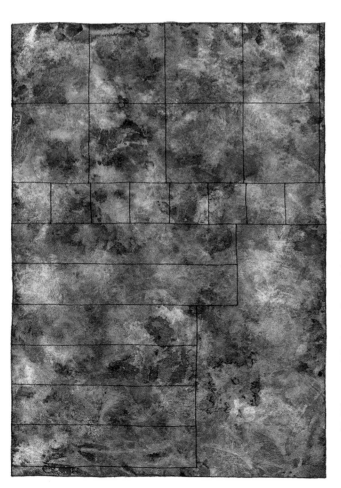

CUTTING

1 Following diagram 1, from the blue fabric, cut eight 12½ in/31.5 cm squares, eight 6½ in/16.5 cm squares, two 6½ x 36½ in/16.5 x 91.5 cm rectangles and four 6½ x 30½ in/16.5 x 76.5 cm strips. Join these last four strips into pairs with a ¼ in/0.75 cm seam to make two strips 6½ x 60½ in/16.5 x 151.5 cm.

2 Cut the same from the orange fabric, except you only need seven 12½ in/31.5 cm squares. Join the strips as before.

STITCHING

1 Referring to the quilt plan, stitch the large squares into rows, then stitch the rows together. Press the seams open.

2 Stitch pairs of rectangles together, one orange to one blue, following the quilt plan.

3 Stitch the longer rectangles to the quilt top sides, matching centres.

4 Stitch together the smaller squares into sets of four and stitch these to each end of the shorter rectangles. Attach these to both ends of the quilt. Press all the seams open.

FINISHING THE QUILT

1 Layer the backing, wadding and quilt top and either use safety pins or baste into a grid system.

2 Machine-quilt with blue thread in straight lines 1 in/2.5 cm on either side of each seam line.

3 Trace off the larger star shape pattern (on page 139) and stick it to the card. Mark round it randomly onto the quilt top 10 to 21 times (depending on time available) and stitch on the marked lines with orange thread.

4 Trace off the smaller star pattern (on page 139) and cut out 10 to 21 stars in felt using freezer paper (see page 142). Pin these stars inside the quilted star motifs and stitch down with blue thread using a straight stitch.

5 Trim the wadding to the same size as the top and trim the backing 1 in/2.5 cm bigger all round. Turn in ½ in/1 cm and fold over onto the quilt top. Machine stitch in place.

TEMPLATES FOR "DUSK" AND "CATCH A FALLING STAR"

Instructions for using the "Dusk" templates below appear on page 138.
Instructions for using the "Catch a Falling Star" templates below appear on page 142.

A = small star (Catch a Falling Star)
B = medium star (Catch a Falling Star)
C = small star (Dusk)
D = large star (Catch a Falling Star and Dusk)

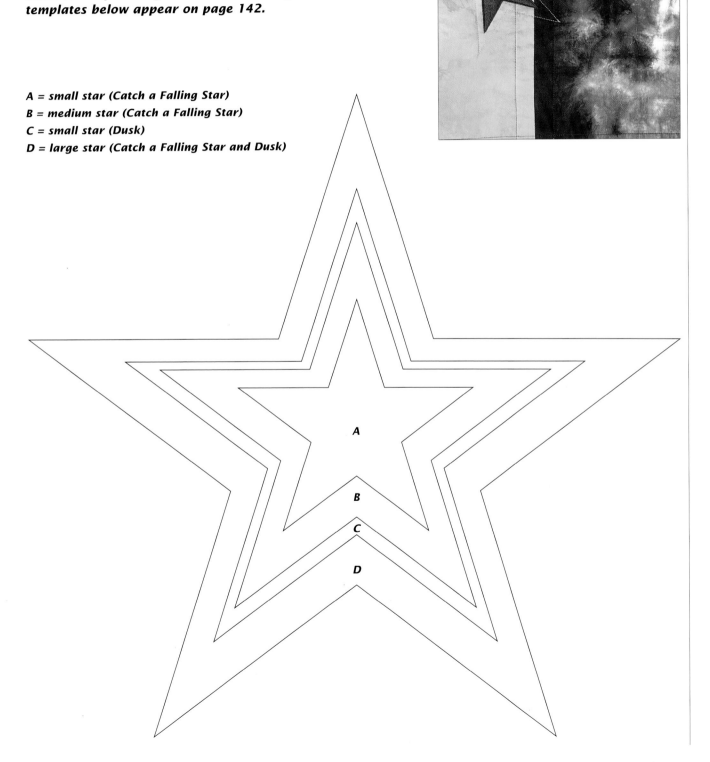

CATCH A FALLING STAR

This cot quilt is made using two layers of a washable acrylic fabric called Kunin felt, without wadding. Patterns cut from felt do not fray and can be stitched in place without a turning. I machine-stitched throughout and it took roughly eight hours to make. This felt is not suitable for constant washing but the quilt could be used more as a decorative top for a pram or cot. By adding a hanging sleeve, it could be used as a nursery wall-hanging.

Quilt size: 34 x 24 in/90 x 60 cm

MATERIALS

Kunin felt (used for the top, backing and some stars): pale yellow, 1¼ yards/115 cm; bright yellow, 1 yard/90 cm; blue, 12 in/30 cm, all 36 in/90 cm wide
Thin card for star templates
Two cotton printed star fabrics (for the large stars): one 8 in/20 cm square from each fabric
Fusible webbing: 8 x 16 in/20 x 40 cm piece

Thicker "top-stitch" thread: pale yellow, bright yellow and blue to match the colours of the felt
Freezer paper
Silicone or baking parchment paper
Rayon machine thread: in colours to match the printed star fabrics
Regular sewing thread: in colours to match the "top-stitching" thread and the rayon machine thread

CUTTING

1 From the pale yellow felt, cut a 34 x 24 in/90 x 60 cm rectangle for the backing.

2 Cut a rectangle the same size from the bright yellow felt for the top layer.

3 Trace off the three star shape patterns on page 139 and stick onto card to use as templates.

4 From the blue felt, cut eight small stars and six medium stars.

5 From bright yellow felt, cut four small stars and four medium stars.

6 From the pale yellow felt, cut eight small stars and eight medium stars.

7 From each of the star fabrics, cut one large star, then iron fusible webbing onto both stars.

STITCHING

1 Baste the two rectangles of felt together and, using matching thicker thread, stitch two rows around the edges, the first row ⅛ in/4 mm from the edge and the second ⅜ in/1 cm from the edge as shown on the quilt plan.

2 Draw round the large star template onto freezer paper and cut out five stars. Following the quilt plan or in your own arrangement, iron them onto the quilt top, using silicone or baking parchment paper to protect the felt. Stitch around the papers using the thicker thread to match the bright yellow felt, then remove.

3 Place the two large fabric stars, just slightly offset from the stitching as shown on the quilt plan. Iron in place, protecting the surface with silicone or baking parchment paper.

4 Satin stitch by machine round the two stars using a rayon thread, or attach by hand with buttonhole stitch.

5 Place the small and medium felt stars at random over the top, trying not to overlap, securing each with a pin.

6 With a darning foot and feed dog down, on each of the stars stitch a spiral from the centre outwards using a contrasting thicker thread (diagram 1).

1

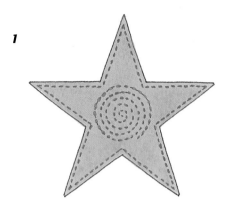

7 Using regular matching coloured thread, stitch down each star with a straight machine stitch around the edges.

FINISHING THE QUILT

1 Using silicone or baking parchment paper to protect the surface, press with a cool iron.

2 Whenever necessary, wash the quilt gently in warm water and dry flat.

USEFUL ADDRESSES

UNITED KINGDOM

Berol
Old Meadow Road
Kings Lynn
Norfolk PE30 4JR
(Suppliers of Pressprint & Easiprint
for fabric printing)

Binney & Smith Ltd
Ampthill Road
Bedford MK42 9RS
(Suppliers of Liquitex acrylic paints)

Dylon International Ltd
Worsley Bridge Road
Lower Sydenham
London SE26 5HD
(0181) 663 4801
(Suppliers of dyes and Cold Fix)

G & G Quilt Company
52 Swan Lane
Coventry CV2 4GB
(01203) 227011
(Suppliers of "Warm and Natural"
cotton wadding)

Groves & Banks
Windsor Road
Redditch
Worcs B97 6DJ
(0527) 591081
(Wholesale supplier of rotary cutters)

Piecemakers
13 Manor Green Road
Epsom Surrey KT19 8RA
(01372) 743161
(Specialist retailer and suppliers of
Kunin felt)

Polly's Patch
19 Water Lane
Cromford
Matlock DE4 3QH
(0629) 825 062
(Specialist retailer)

The Quilt Room
c/o Carvilles
Station Road
Dorking Surrey RH4 1HQ
(01306) 877307
(Mail order)

The Quilt Room
20 West Street
Dorking Surrey RH4 1BL
(01306) 740739
(Specialist Retail)

AUSTRALIA

Patchwork Plus
Shop 20, 282 Forest Road
Hurstville NSW 2220
(02) 580 2486

The Quilting Bee
14 Gordon Village Arcade
Gordon NSW 2072
(02) 499 2203

Patchwork Addicition
1087 Mt Alexander Road
Essendon North
VICTORIA 3041
(03) 379 6792

Quilts and Threads
1015 Lower North East Road
Highbury
SOUTH AUSTRALIA 5089
(08) 396 3711

Riverlea Cottage Quilts
330 Unley Road
Hyde Park
SOUTH AUSTRALIA 5061
(08) 373 0653

Country Patchwork Cottage
86 Erindale Road
Balcatta
WESTERN
AUSTRALIA 6021
(09) 345 3550

Patchwork Supplies
43 Gloucester Street
Highgate Hill
QUEENSLAND 4101
(07) 844 9391

The Quilter's Store
22 Shaw Street
Auchenflower
QUEENSLAND 4066
(07) 870 0408

NEW ZEALAND

Patches of Ponsonby
101 Ponsonby Road
Ponsonby
Auckland
(376) 1556

Patchwork Barn
132 Hinemoa Street
Birkenhead
Auckland
(480) 5401

Patchwork & Quilting
Fabrics & Supplies
Shop 19
Manukau City Shopping Centre
Manukau City
(262) 1757

Daydreams
PO Box 69072
Glendene
Auckland
(837) 0019

Grandmothers Garden Patchwork
Shop
7/100 Wellington Street
Ponsonby
(378) 8899

Manurewa Handcraft Supplies
Arcade Station Road
Manurewa
(266) 9040

Masco Ltd
229 Karangahope Road
Auckland
(379) 3500

Past Time Quilting & Embroidery
13a Cromwell Street
Hendersen
(838) 9710

SOUTH AFRICA

Crafty Supplies
32 Main Road
Claremont
Cape Town
7700
(Retail and mail order)
Tel: (021) 61 0286
Fax: (021) 61 0308

Pickles & Patchwork
97 Howard Centre
Pinelands
Cape Town
7405
Tel: (021) 531 0617
Fax: (021) 531 9440

Bernina Sew & Knit
53 Sanlam Plaza
Maitland Street
Bloemfontein
9301

Needlewoman
Sharma Plaza
Charles Street
Bloemfontein
9301

IMPORTERS FROM THE UK AND
USA:
Mrs Morrow or Norma Morrow
Umbilo Drapers
684 Umbilo Road
Durban
4001
Tel: (031) 25 7814

Bernina Sew & Knit
Southdale Shopping Centre
Southdale
Johannesburg
2091
Tel: (011) 433 3551

Doreen's Work Basket
Shop 91A
Westgate Shopping Centre
Roodepoort
Johannesburg
1724
Tel/Fax: (011) 764 5305

Pied Piper
13 Kemsley Street
Central
Port Elizabeth
6001

ACKNOWLEDGEMENTS

Quilters often rely on the pioneering work of others in developing new ideas. We would like to thank those who have kindly given us permission to reproduce their designs:

Patchwork Quilt Tsushin for permission to use Sawako Tsurugiji's kimono block design in Jenni Dobson's "Pacific Kimono".

That Patchwork Place for allowing us to use the quilting stitches in Gill Turley's "Decorative Stitch Sampler". The quilting stitch patterns are copyrighted designs by Judy D. Hopkins and published in "Rotary Riot" by Judy Hopkins and Nancy J. Martin, published by That Patchwork Place, 1991. They also produce the "BiRangle".

INDEX